WHAT NURSES KNOW...

P T S D

WHAT NURSES KNOW...

PTSD

Mary E. Muscari, PhD, RN WITHDRAWN

 demos HEALTH

New York

Visit our website at www.demoshealth.com
ISBN: 978-1-936303-06-9
e-book ISBN: 978-1-617050-51-0

Acquisitions Editor: Noreen Henson
Compositor: Newgen
Printer: Hamilton Printing

Medical information provided by Demos Health, in the absence of a visit with a health care professional, must be considered as an educational service only. This book is not designed to replace a physician's independent judgment about the appropriateness or risks of a procedure or therapy for a given patient. Our purpose is to provide you with information that will help you make your own health care decisions.

The information and opinions provided here are believed to be accurate and sound, based on the best judgment available to the authors, editors, and publisher, but readers who fail to consult appropriate health authorities assume the risk of injuries. The publisher is not responsible for errors or omissions. The editors and publisher welcome any reader to report to the publisher any discrepancies or inaccuracies noticed.

Library of Congress Cataloging-in-Publication Data
CIP data is available from the Library of Congress.

Special discounts on bulk quantities of Demos Health books are available to corporations, professional associations, pharmaceutical companies, health care organizations, and other qualifying groups. For details, please contact:

Special Sales Department
Demos Medical Publishing, LLC
11 West 42nd Street, 15th Floor
New York, NY 10036
Phone: 800-532-8663 or 212-683-0072
Fax: 212-941-7842
E-mail: rsantana@demosmedpub.com

Made in the United States of America
12 13 14 15   5 4 3 2 1

About the Author

Mary E. Muscari, PhD, RN, is Associate Professor at the Decker School of Nursing, Binghamton University (NY), and Affiliate Faculty in the Department of Criminology at Regis University (CO). She continues to use her experience in pediatric, psychiatric, and forensic nursing in both her clinical practice and her writing, particularly regarding victims and perpetrators of violence. She has written numerous articles and several books, including *Everything Parents Guide to Raising Adolescent Girls; Everything Parents Guide to Raising Adolescent Boys* (both 2008 from Adams Media with lead authors Moira McCarthy and Robin Elise Weiss, respectively); *Let Kids be Kids: Rescuing Childhood* (2006); *Not My Kid: 21 Steps to Raising a Nonviolent Kid* (2002); and *Not My Kid 2: Protecting Your Children from the 21 Threats of the 21st Century* (2004) (all from University of Scranton Press). She has been interviewed by many national publications, including *Parents Magazine, Family Circle, The Christian Science Monitor, Better Homes & Gardens, USA Today, The Philadelphia Inquirer,* and the *Los Angeles Times.*

WHAT NURSES KNOW...

Nurses hold a critical role in modern healthcare that goes beyond their day-to-day duties. They share more information with patients than any other provider group, and are alongside patients twenty-four hours a day, seven days a week, offering understanding of complex health issues, holistic approaches to ailments, and advice for the patient that extends to the family. Nurses themselves are a powerful tool in the healing process.

What Nurses Know gives down-to-earth information, addresses consumers as equal partners in their care, and explains clearly what readers need to know and want to know to understand their condition and move forward with their lives.

This book is dedicated to all my fur-babies, past and present, who wait patiently while I spend time at my computer.

Contents

x　●　●　●　Contents

Foreword

PTSD transforms millions of people who have been affected by violence, war, natural disasters, and other traumatic events. Their lives can be upset by a roller-coaster ride of emotions that can interfere with their day-to-day living, including how they relate to their family and friends.

If you or your loved one has PTSD, *What Nurses Know... PTSD* can help you manage symptoms and help you along on your path to wellness. This book is written in a user-friendly manner that will allow you to either read it cover to cover or just choose the information that works best for you. It is especially helpful if you have been a victim of abuse or assault, but it is equally helpful if you have experienced a flood, accident, and other traumatic loss, or if your partner or child has PTSD. You will better understand this problem, its symptoms, and its treatments, but, most importantly, you will realize that you are not alone in your struggle, that there are many people out there who are going through the same difficulties and many who are willing to help.

Ann Wolbert Burgess, DNS, RNCS, FAAN
Professor
William F. Connell School of Nursing
Boston College

Preface

"My husband was in Iraq in 2004-2005, where he was stationed on the border and worked as an MP that escorted convoys through Iraq. He now has a mild case of PTSD, but it was worse when he first came home. The three areas he has the most problems with are sleeping, being out in crowds, and driving. He also was getting daily, severe, and constant headaches. He has trouble concentrating when he reads, and tends to end up reading the same line over and over, which frustrates him. He has not slept a full night since he got back, sometimes having violent nightmares that bring him back to Iraq. I know whenever we go out to eat in a restaurant, he won't sit with his back to the door, so I always know to take that seat first. When we are out in crowds, he is always constantly scanning, checking the crowd. He is always on heightened alert when driving too, especially when passing other vehicles on his right... always looking for the end of a gun sticking out the window at him. When he first got home, he was a very aggressive driver, scaring people that rode in the vehicle with him. He had been used to driving that way, just trying to survive over there and it took him a while to calm down when driving here at home. As a nurse, I have tried to get him to open up about his experiences a little at a time, when he is ready. It has been a slow process. He is just now going to the VA to get help, 6 years later. He is talking to the counselors there, but that is a frustrating process in itself, with many appointments that he has to leave work for. They also like to fix problems by throwing a lot of medications at them. For his sleep problems, they gave him Trazodone, which is actually an antidepressant, with side effects of increased hostility and aggression. He insisted he is not depressed (which is true). My husband is a big man, trained to kill people, so the thought of giving him a medicine that might make him more hostile and aggressive didn't sound like a good idea to either of us. So he never took it. He did go to a chiropractor for his headaches, and that has helped a lot. Since he doesn't like taking medications, I suggested he try acupuncture to help him with the sleeping problems, and he is considering it, but hasn't gone yet. I have been trying to help him deal with all of his issues, but it is a slow process. I feel blessed that his PTSD is mild, but I worry about the many other returning servicemen and women who are really struggling with it. There needs to be more help available to them, especially with the rise of suicides in returning veterans. There is a local family with two twin brothers, both went to combat ... one came home a Wounded Warrior with a loss of a limb, the other one, set to deploy again, committed suicide. He left behind a wife and three children. It is so heartbreaking. We are failing our veterans and servicemen and women, and they need our help. Freedom is not free, it comes with a cost and a price and many American men and women (and their families) are paying that price. We need to do better."–Carol

Posttraumatic stress disorder (PTSD) affects almost 5.2 million adults during a given year. This potentially debilitating illness occurs when a person is exposed to a dangerous, terrifying, possibly life-threatening event. It can interfere with your relationships, your work, and your social life.

Although most commonly associated with the military (post-deployment syndrome), PTSD can develop when any person experiences an extremely traumatic event that is considered beyond normal human experience, including sexual assault, the sudden death of a loved one, a hurricane, or a terrorist bombing. The term "traumatic event" can also be relative—what's traumatic to one person may not be traumatic to another. Thus, people can suffer PTSD from events that are less catastrophic, including unemployment or divorce. Furthermore, the effects of PTSD are far reaching since the disorder can also affect family members, friends, and co-workers.

This book is designed to help you learn more about PTSD, whether it affects you, your spouse/partner, or your child. First and foremost, you need to know if you truly have PTSD. Trauma affects us all in different ways. People normally feel a wide range of emotions after experiencing or witnessing a traumatic event. You may feel fear, anxiety, or sadness; you may have changes in your eating or sleeping patterns; and you may have nightmares or recurrent thoughts about the event. But these do not necessarily mean that you have PTSD.

This book helps victims and their families recognize the problem of PTSD and know how and where to get assistance. It answers questions about: the causes of PTSD, the symptoms, the effect it has on victims and their loved ones, associated problems such as substance abuse, what makes PTSD different in children and adolescents, how to manage stress, how to talk to your health care provider about PTSD, and how to get help—both traditional and nontraditional sources.

While this book can be a valuable resource if you or a loved one has PTSD, it is not meant to take the place of therapy. If the symptoms of PTSD interfere with your daily routine or your relationships, you should initiate and maintain a therapeutic relationship with a counselor. If you do not have one, Chapter 5 will help you find one. If your symptoms are so severe that you think about hurting yourself or someone else, call 911 or your local emergency service.

Chapter 1 describes PTSD and differentiates it from similar disorders. PTSD is an anxiety disorder characterized by specific symptoms that develop following exposure to an extremely stressful event. The event involves real or threatened death, serious injury or another treat to the person's physical integrity. This event may have been experienced directly, witnessed, or learned through a third party. While PTSD may be similar to other anxiety disorders, it is not the same as acute stress disorder, obsessive compulsive disorder, and adjustment disorder, nor is it a brief psychotic disorder or Stockholm syndrome, and this chapter shows you the differences.

Chapter 2 discusses why you may have developed PTSD. Researchers are still working to understand the causes of PTSD; however, most mental illnesses have various causes, and PTSD is probably no different. Thus, PTSD is most likely a combination of four elements: inherited predisposition to mental illness, particularly anxiety (including PTSD) and depression; life experience that includes frequency and severity of traumas since childhood; your personality or temperament; and how your brain regulates your body's response to stress.

Chapter 3 explains your symptoms and Chapter 4 talks about the long-term effects of PTSD. Symptoms generally begin within three months of the trauma; however, symptoms may be delayed as long as months or years for some people. Symptoms may wax and wane or even disappear completely. Regardless of duration, symptoms tend to fall into three categories: persistent re-experiencing of the event, persistent avoidance of stimuli related to the event, and persistent symptoms of increased arousal. Many people with PTSD have other psychiatric problems, particularly depression, substance abuse, and other anxiety disorders. The symptoms of PTSD, with or without the presence of a co-existing disorder, can create havoc on the person's relationships, job, and other life aspects. PTSD alone causes significant distress or impairment in social, occupational, or other important areas of functioning.

As an anxiety disorder, PTSD is associated with stress, and stress is associated with physical health problems, including cardiovascular disease, chronic pain, autoimmune diseases, and musculoskeletal conditions. Finally, since PTSD resulted from trauma, persons with this disorder may also suffer from other aspects of victimization or the aftermath of disaster.

The next two chapters, Chapters 5 and 6, discuss the traditional and alternative treatments for PTSD, respectively. There are many treatments for PTSD and its associated problems, but the main approaches are support, encouragement to discuss the event, and education about a variety of coping mechanisms. The emphasis is usually on education about the disorder and its treatment. The main treatment methods are psychotherapy, medications, or a combination of both. Complementary and Alternative Medicine (CAM) approaches to the treatment have been utilized for many medical and mental health diagnoses, including PTSD, even though the research base to support their effectiveness is not complete but is improving.

Chapter 7 enables you to work better with your primary care provider and therapist to combat your PTSD. They are your mentors in your journey to healing and wellness. But you need to know how to make the best of these working relationships.

Chapter 8 helps you deal with stress in general, a critical ability when you have PTSD.

Stress overload can challenge your ability to care for yourself, your family, and your job. It can also cause stress-related disorders. Stress-related conditions can lead to poor work performance or even injury, as well as various biological reactions that may lead ultimately to compromised health, such as cardiovascular disease. Stress is also expensive. Chronic stress leads to feelings of being "stressed out" or "burned out." Stress may not be easy to recognize because it often affects the body, leading one to believe that he or she is ill rather than stressed.

Chapter 9 is for those whose partner has PTSD. Your partner's PTSD can strain your relationship, your mental health, and your family. Compared to veterans without PTSD, veterans with PTSD have more marital troubles. They share less of their thoughts and feelings and they have intimacy problems, as sexual problems tend to be higher in combat veterans with PTSD. The National Vietnam Veterans Readjustment Study (NVVRS) compared veterans with PTSD to those without PTSD and found the following in Vietnam veterans with PTSD: They got divorced twice as much; were three times more likely to divorce two or more times; and tended to have shorter relationships.

Chapter 10 helps you deal with your child's PTSD. Severe trauma can undermine children's sense of security and cause them to believe that their parents cannot protect them from harm. Traumatized youth are frequently preoccupied with danger and vulnerability, which can sometimes lead to misperceptions of danger, even in situations that are not threatening. Several studies have shown that once posttraumatic stress symptoms emerge, PTSD leads to neurophysiologic correlates that impact brain function in developing children and adolescents.

A resource list and glossary follows the chapters. The resource list contains the names and contact information of various agencies that may be useful to you during your journey. The glossary helps you understand words and phrases that relate to PTSD.

Each chapter, and this preface, begins with a brief story from someone who either suffers from PTSD or whose family member had the disorder. Given the significance of the content of their stories, pseudonyms were used instead of real names. However, I applaud and thank these brave women for their courage in being able to share their journeys with us.

Acknowledgments

I would like to thank Editors Noreen Henson and Margaret Zuccarini for their support in developing this book, and I appreciate the help of the Demos team (Tom Hastings, Rose Mary Piscitelli, and Ashita Shah).

Thanks also go to the readers, especially those who have bravely fought PTSD. I wish you all the best on your journey to healing and wellness. I especially thank the brave women who shared their PTSD stories with us. It took a tremendous amount of courage to come forward to help others who also suffer from PTSD or who have loved ones with PTSD.

I would like to thank the following people who contributed to this book: Anh Ung, BA, Data Analyst at Memorial Sloan-Kettering Cancer Center (NY) (Chapter 9); Won Joo Christina Yoon, Nursing Student Class of 2011 at the Decker School of Nursing, Binghamton University (NY) (Chapter 6 and PTSD Resources Section); Jane Jungah Park, Nursing Student Class of

2011 at the Decker School of Nursing, Binghamton University (NY) (Chapter 1); Eunice A. Ochuonyo, Nursing Student Class of 2011 at the Decker School of Nursing, Binghamton University (NY) (Chapter 9); Jean Van Kingsley, MS, RN, FNP-BC, board-certified Family Nurse Practitioner at the New York State Veterans' Home in Oxford, New York, with over 10 years of experience guiding veterans of the armed services and their families through end-of-life decisions (Poem in Chapter 9).

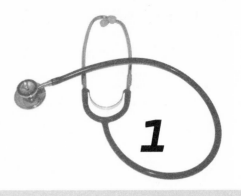

PTSD: What It Is and Isn't

Survivor's feelings as a young person: *"Emotionally shut down. Bone-deep dread of abuser. Physical revulsion of self and father. Feeling like a piece of meat. Feeling like my father had a religious, God-given right to my body. Inability to enforce personal boundaries. Personally sinful, dirty, useless, and unimportant. Unable to develop personal power. Encapsulated and frozen. Distorted body image. Helpless and hopeless. Fear of failure and fear of success. Fear of almost everything, especially of going to hell. Unable to take risks. Suicidal thoughts to escape the pain. Constantly hearing 'You are the fruit of my loins' (what a repulsive expression!). Rage (carefully controlled) when hearing that abused persons become abusers themselves. I'd rather die than abuse anyone. I know the pain."* ABBY

In the movie *Groundhog Day*, weatherman Phil Connor reluctantly sets out to cover Punxsutawney Phil's annual prediction of winter's end. He plans to get the story and go, but a snow storm traps him in the tiny Pennsylvania town. When he awakens the next day, it's déjà vu, and he ends up repeating that February 2nd over and over again, stuck in the same place with the same people, perpetually experiencing the same events. At first, Phil doesn't know how to handle his dilemma. He tries to cope by using what worked for him in the past, but gets nowhere. Then things begin to change, and Phil finally wakes up to a brand new day.

If you have posttraumatic stress disorder (PTSD), you're a lot like Phil in *Groundhog Day*, stuck in a time warp, reliving the same event over and over again. However, unlike Phil, you don't have Hollywood magic and thus can't turn your life around in a commercial-free 101 minutes. But your life is still your story, complete with plot twists and a cast of characters – some are friends and mentors, others are villains. No matter the course, you are the hero of your story, and all heroes must face crises that force them to change over the course of time. Your story deserves a happy ending, but to get there you need to learn not only how to cope with PTSD, but how to move beyond it and become an

What Nurses Know . . .

Learning about your disorder is enlightening and empowering, but it can also be stressful. If you begin to feel anxious while reading this book, put it down, take some deep breaths, and imagine yourself in a safe, comforting place. Should your anxiety escalate at any time, contact your therapist immediately.

even better person than the one you were before tragedy struck. This book will help you find your way along the hero's journey, a trip made famous by writers Joseph Campbell (*The Hero with a Thousand Faces*) and Chris Vogler (*The Writer's Journey: Mythic Structure for Writers*). Their heroes are fictional, and reality is far more difficult and unpredictable, but the rewards are so much sweeter when we work hard to achieve them.

The Journey Begins

First and foremost, please know that you are not "crazy," even though you may feel that way at times. You may have persistent frightening memories of your terrible ordeal, startle at familiar sights and sounds, and feel emotionally numb with those who matter most. But you are not drifting in and out of psychosis – you are simply struggling with PTSD. You are not weak: PTSD is a response to a significantly traumatic event where specific chemical changes in your brain occurred in response to that event. And you are not alone: The National Center for PTSD notes that almost 5.2 million adults have PTSD during a given year.

You have a real illness, one that is as real as high blood pressure or diabetes, and one that creates real physiologic problems. Don't let anyone tell you otherwise. Although the stigma of mental illness has diminished greatly, some people remain callous toward those who face the challenges that come from these disorders, including PTSD. Such people's judgments usually flow from their lack of understanding and reliance on urban myths rather than facts. One of the best ways to overcome stigmatizing of PTSD is for you to come to terms with it yourself. There's no more reason to be ashamed of PTSD than there is to be ashamed of asthma, heart disease, or any other chronic illness.

Your personal struggle with PTSD is part of your story. While it may seem insurmountable at times, it does not define you as a person. PTSD is merely a barrier in your journey, and you need to learn to either walk around it or plow right through it to get back onto the path of healthy living.

A successful journey begins with a plan, and this book is your plan. It does not take the place of treatment, but counseling alone does not seem to help people get past their trauma. Thus, this book complements your treatment counseling and serves as the map for your journey. Your successful journey begins in this chapter where you will learn what PTSD is, and what it is not.

PTSD: What It Is

PTSD is a potentially debilitating illness that occurs when a person is exposed to a dangerous, terrifying, possibly life-threatening event. It is an anxiety disorder that can interfere with your relationships, your work, and your social life. Although most commonly associated with the military (post-deployment syndrome), PTSD can develop when a person experiences an extremely traumatic event that is considered beyond normal human experience, including sexual assault, the sudden death of a loved one, a hurricane, or a terrorist bombing. The term "traumatic event" is relative - what is traumatic to one person may not be traumatic to another. Thus, people can suffer PTSD from events such as unemployment or divorce.

Trauma affects us all in different ways. People normally feel a wide range of emotions after experiencing or witnessing a traumatic event. You may feel fear, anxiety or sadness; you

What Nurses Know ...

PTSD can be treated. Treatment usually includes talking with a therapist (psychotherapy), medications (psychopharmacology), or a combination of both.

may have changes in your eating or sleeping patterns; and you may have nightmares or recurrent thoughts about the event. But these do not necessarily mean that you have PTSD. With PTSD, you brain stays in overdrive long after the trauma, working in a hyperalert state waiting for the next potential trauma. You may experience flashbacks and nightmares, or you may feel numb and try to avoid circumstances that remind you of the trauma.

PTSD is the great pretender. Thus, the first major stumbling block in your journey is that PTSD often goes unrecognized. Primary healthcare providers (doctors, nurse practitioners, and physician assistants) may not be aware of - or ask about - the symptoms, even after someone has experienced trauma. Surprisingly, many primary healthcare providers receive minimal education on mental illness, and even fewer learn about the effects of trauma and victimization. Another barrier is that persons with PTSD may not tell their providers about traumatic events. This is especially true of the trauma of sexual abuse, child abuse, and intimate partner violence (also called domestic violence) because these are very painful to talk about. If a person does not reveal the trauma, the diagnosis becomes difficult to make. People with PTSD may also have other disorders, such as substance abuse or depression, which may have symptoms that overlap those of PTSD. If you have yet to discuss the possibility of PTSD with your healthcare provider, do so soon. If you are not sure how to approach your provider, Chapter 7 will help you with that. And, if you are not sure if you have PTSD, take that the mini quiz on the following page.

PTSD is an anxiety disorder that is characterized by specific symptoms that develop following exposure to an extremely stressful event. The event usually involves real or threatened death, serious injury, or another treat to the person's physical integrity. This event may have been experienced directly, or witnessed or learned through a third party. For example, the person may have experienced abuse directly, witnessed it,

DO I HAVE PTSD?

Professionals have difficulty diagnosing PTSD, so it is not surprising that that you too may be unsure whether or not you have it.

		Yes	No
1	Did you experience a traumatic event more than one month ago?		
2	Do you have flashbacks about the event?		
3	Do you have nightmares about the event?		
4	Do you feel constantly on guard or watchful?		
5	Are you easily startled?		
6	Do you feel numb and unable to feel emotion?		
7	Do you feel detached from the people around you?		
8	Do you try to avoid people, places, events or things that remind you of the trauma?		
9	Did the above problems begin after the traumatic event?		

If you said "yes" to questions 1 and 9, as well as three or more of the other questions, you may have PTSD.

or heard about the abuse of a family member or close associate. The person's reaction to the traumatic event involves intense horror, fear, or helplessness. Symptoms involve persistently reliving the trauma, persistently avoiding things that are associated with the trauma, a general numbing of responsiveness that did not exist before the trauma, and persistent symptoms of arousal. Persistence of these reactions is the key to a diagnosis of PTSD; symptoms must be present for more than one month and cause either significant distress or

What Nurses Know...

PTSD can be difficult to diagnose. Symptoms may mimic other disorders, and many people who have PTSD have another co-occurring disorder.

impairment in the person's personal, family, social, school, or occupational life. The characteristics of PTSD are somewhat different in children, but these will be discussed in detail in Chapter 10.

What Is the History of PTSD?

Although PTSD is relatively new as a recognized psychiatric disorder, writers have described it as far back as ancient times, expressing their understanding that exposure to terrifying and life-threatening events leaves a lasting impression on the human mind, body, and soul.

- *Circa 5000 B.C.:* Possibly the earliest description of the symptoms of PTSD is seen in the Indian epic *Ramayana*, written by Maharshi Valmiki. According to this epic story, Marrich had symptoms of PTSD after he was grievously hurt by Lord Rama's arrow and was almost killed. This trauma threatened his physical integrity and caused him to develop all the symptoms of PTSD, including hyperarousal, re-experiencing the event, and avoidance.
- *720 B.C.:* Homer wrote what could be described as PTSD in the rage of Achilles after the death of his friend Patroclus.
- *1800s:* Military doctors began diagnosing soldiers with "exhaustion" following battle stress. During that same time, doctors in England noted a syndrome knows then as "railway

spine" or "railway hysteria." This syndrome bore a striking resemblance to PTSD, and was exhibited by people who had been in the catastrophic railway accidents of the period.

- *American Civil War (1861-1865):* Dr. Mendez DaCosta published a paper diagnosing Civil War veterans with "soldiers heart." Symptoms included startle responses, hypervigilance, and irregular heartbeat.
- *World War I (1914-1919):* "Combat fatigue" and "shell shock" were the labels for those soldiers who experienced PTSD symptoms in World War I.
- *World War II (1939-1945):* The labels "battle fatigue" and "gross stress reaction" were applied to soldiers with PTSD symptoms in World War II.
- *1952:* PTSD was first recognized as a psychiatric disorder called "stress response syndrome," which was caused by "gross stress reaction."
- *1960s-1970s:* Independent research teams studied the experiences of Holocaust survivors, survivors of rape, battered children, burn victims, and Vietnam veterans. These researchers developed separate pockets of knowledge about particular types of traumas, but it was not until the 1970s that links were made among them.
- *1980:* Prior to the studies conducted on Vietnam veterans, there was little research of what we today call PTSD. The

What Nurses Know...

The term "posttraumatic stress disorder" was first used after the Vietnam War. PTSD was officially recognized as a mental illness when it was included in the Diagnostic and Statistical Manual of Mental Disorders, *developed by the American Psychiatric Association (APA).*

official diagnosis of posttraumatic stress disorder appeared in 1980.

- *1987-1994:* The definition of "traumatic event" changed to include events not outside the range of usual human experience, such as automobile accidents.

Who Gets PTSD?

Anyone can develop PTSD, including children, since many people suffer some form of trauma. Approximately 60% of men and 50% of women experience at least one trauma during their lives. Men are more likely to experience physical assault, combat, disaster, or accidents, or to witness death or injury, while women are more likely to experience child sexual abuse or an adult sexual assault. Experiencing trauma does not automatically equate to PTSD, and, in fact, while the number of those who suffer from PTSD is large, those with PTSD represent only a small percent of persons who have suffered trauma. However, the numbers of people with PTSD are still astounding. More than five million adults have PTSD during a given year; and 7% to 8% of the population will develop PTSD. And while men may experience more traumas, women are more likely to develop PTSD, with about 10% of women developing PTSD in their lifetimes compared to 5% of men.

Although anyone can develop PTSD, some people are more at risk than others. When you completed the *Do I have PTSD?* questionnaire, you probably had one or more of the risk factors prior to developing PTSD. Being female places you at risk, as does being young. Exposure to previous traumatic events, having minimal support from family and friends, having experienced a recent significant loss or other stressful life event, having other mental health problems, and abusing alcohol place people at risk, as does having a family member with PTSD or depression. The traumatic event experience can increase risk if you: were seriously hurt; thought the trauma was severe or

What Nurses Know...

Are you at risk to develop PTSD? The National Center for PTSD notes that women are more likely to develop PTSD if they:
- *Had a past mental health problem, such as anxiety or depression*
- *Experienced a very severe or life-threatening trauma*
- *Were sexually assaulted*
- *Were injured during the trauma*
- *Had a severe reaction at the time of the trauma*
- *Experienced other stressful events after the trauma*
- *Do not have good social support*

long-lasting; believed you or a family member were in danger; felt helpless; or if you had a severe reaction during the event, such as vomiting or feeling surreal.

What Are the Symptoms of PTSD?

PTSD can cause multitude of symptoms, which can be grouped into three categories. They are outlined here and explained in detail in Chapter 3:

1. *Re-experiencing symptoms*: Intrusive memories of the trauma; flashbacks (reliving the trauma over and over); bad dreams; and frightening thoughts. Re-experiencing symptoms may interfere with your everyday routine.
2. *Avoidance symptoms*: Staying away from people, places, events, or objects that are reminders of the experience; not being able to remember significant aspects of the trauma; showing a limited range of emotion; feeling emotionally

numb; feeling guilt, depression, or worry; losing interest in activities that were once pleasurable activities; and having a sense of a shortened future. These symptoms may cause a person to change his or her personal routine.

3. *Hyperarousal symptoms*: Being easily startled; feeling tense or "on edge"; having difficulty sleeping; and having angry outbursts. Hyperarousal symptoms are usually constant instead of being triggered by things that remind one of the traumatic events. These symptoms can make it hard to do daily tasks, such as sleeping, eating, or concentrating.

How Is PTSD Diagnosed?

PTSD may sound like a straightforward problem; however, diagnosis is difficult, and the disorder often goes unrecognized. PTSD is unique among psychiatric disorders because it is identified by its symptoms, as well as the precipitating event. The diagnosis requires that specific criteria be met:

- The person was exposed to a traumatic event whereby the person experienced, witnessed, or was confronted with an event that involved actual or threatened death or serious injury to the person or others, and the person's response to the trauma involved intense fear, helplessness, or horror.
- The person has characteristics of all three symptom clusters outlined in the previous section.
- The symptoms have lasted at least one month in duration.
- The symptoms cause significant distress or impairment in social, occupational, or other important areas of function.

To make the diagnosis, your healthcare professional will ask you many questions about your current, past, and family histories, and will also ask about the traumatizing event. While you do not need to go into detail at this time, it is critical that you tell your healthcare professional enough about the trauma to enable him or her to make the diagnosis. Your healthcare professional may administer one or more PTSD screening tests, which are simply more questions. He or she will also conduct a physical examination, and possibly order blood work and other health-related tests, to make sure you do not have any underlying physical health problems, especially because PTSD can cause you to have physical symptoms, such as chest pain and sweating. Because PTSD can also have co-occurring mental health problems, your healthcare professional may also conduct other types of screening tests or refer you to a specialist who can assist in making the diagnosis. Be patient. This diagnosis can take some time and may not happen in one visit. However, it is critical that you get the right diagnosis to get the right treatment.

Complex PTSD

The term "complex PTSD" was developed by Dr. Judith Herman to describe symptoms experienced by survivors of significant, long-term (months to years) trauma. Dr. Herman notes that the victim is generally held in a state of physical or emotional captivity for a prolonged period of time. The victim is under the control of the perpetrator and unable to flee. Examples of such traumatic situations include: concentration camps, prisoner of war camps, prostitution brothels, long-term domestic violence, long-term child physical abuse, long-term child sexual abuse, and organized child exploitation rings. Treatment of complex PTSD usually takes much longer, may progress at a much slower rate, and requires a highly structured treatment program delivered by a team of trauma specialists.

Sometimes called "disorder of extreme stress," complex PTSD is considered a different disorder from PTSD and can be very debilitating with a more pervasive pattern of symptoms. People with complex PTSD often have been diagnosed with a personality or dissociative disorder, and may exhibit behavior problems

What Nurses Know...

PTSD creates more cost problems than any other anxiety disorder. The cost of care for the 300,000 veterans returning from Iraq and Afghanistan who currently have PTSD is estimated at $4 to $6.2 billion.

(impulsivity, aggression, eating disorders, sexual acting out, drug abuse, and other self-destructive behaviors), extreme emotional difficulties (intense rage or suicidal thoughts), relationship difficulties (isolation, distrust, and repeated search for a rescuer), and altered consciousness (fragmented thoughts, dissociation, amnesia). They may have distorted views of their perpetrator, such as attributing total power to the perpetrator, being preoccupied with the relationship to the perpetrator, and being preoccupied with revenge. Persons with complex PTSD may also experience a loss of sustaining faith or a sense of despair.

PTSD: What It Is Not

PTSD may be confused with other disorders. Although trauma is characteristic of PTSD, it is also a crucial factor in acute stress disorder. Symptoms of avoidance, numbing, and increased arousal are found in PTSD, but are diagnostic of this disorder only when they occur after exposure to a stressor. If they occurred prior to the stressor, another disorder may be present.

DIFFERENCE BETWEEN ANXIETY AND ANXIETY DISORDER

Everyone gets anxious at some time or another. *Anxiety* is a feeling of general uneasiness. It's different from fear. Fear is specific; anxiety is more diffuse. You fear the dark, but the thought of nightfall makes you anxious. Thus, fear also relates to something more concrete and in the moment, while anxiety is more fluid - you can't always put your finger on it. You know you feel uneasy, but you just can't name exactly what it is that's upsetting you. And anxiety is anticipatory, you foresee whatever it is that bothers you and you become anxious in anticipation of it.

Anxiety may be acute or chronic. Acute anxiety is triggered by a change or imminent loss that threatens your sense of security. Human beings' sense of security is critical to our well-being. It is so critical that theorist Abraham Maslow said that our need for safety and security is second only to our need for oxygen, food, and water. Chronic anxiety is a characteristic of one's personality that exists for a long time. People can have low or high levels of either type of anxiety.

Very few people are anxiety free. Anxiety is a normal and necessary emotion. It's part of our survival instinct. It helps trigger that little voice in your head that says, "Something's wrong. Get out of here!" when you enter a potentially dangerous situation. It's that terrible sensation that tells you that your child is ill or injured, even when they are not in front of you. It's that little bit of tension that helps us study for exams, prepare for that important presentation, or get your game on for that big game. Without it you may not push to do your best and fail the examination, blow the promotion, or lose the playoffs. Normal anxiety helps get you through life's challenges. But the key here is the level of anxiety. Anxiety at its finest is anxiety at a low, mild level.

Anxiety may be mild, moderate, or severe or become panic. As just noted, *mild anxiety* is part of day-to-day life. Your ability to perceive reality is brought into sharp focus. You see, hear, and grasp more information, and your problem-solving skills kick into high gear. However, even good anxiety has its discomforts, or it wouldn't be anxiety. You still feel uneasy, restless, tense, or even irritable, and you may become fidgety and twirl your hair, bite your lip, wring your hands, or tap your toes. But these sensations are worth it when you make anxiety work for you instead of against you. Mild anxiety can be very motivating.

When you escalate to *moderate anxiety*, your perception narrows and you begin to miss details. Instead of your senses being heightened, they decrease, and you see, hear, and grasp less information. You may develop selective inattention, noticing only certain things around you or only those things pointed out by others. You can't think as clearly as you normally would. You can still problem solve, but you're not at your best, and you may have to ask questions repeatedly before making sense of the answer. Now you really feel the anxiety. Your voice shakes, your heart begins to pound, and your muscles tense. It gets a little harder to breathe, and the aches and pains seep in along with some insomnia. Moderate anxiety signals that something in your life needs attention, yet it is still a normal part of life.

Severe anxiety decreases your ability to focus to the point that you may get stuck on one tiny detail or many scattered ones. You're lost in your own space and can't notice what's going on around you, even if someone points it out. When you're this dazed and confused, problem solving no longer functions and your behavior becomes automatic in an attempt to relieve or reduce your anxiety. Your heart races, and you hyperventilate. You speech becomes rapid and loud. You may feel a sense of dread or impending doom, or you may become demanding and threatening. The aches and pains intensify, and you may feel nauseated.

Panic is anxiety at its extreme. You simply can't process what's going on. Your speech becomes unintelligible or even nonexistent. You could become extremely hyperactive, aggressive, or psychotic and lose touch with reality, experiencing hallucinations (faulty sensory perceptions, such as hearing voices that are not there) or delusions (false beliefs, such as thinking someone is trying to kill you). Panic can lead to exhaustion and warrants immediate attention because you can hurt yourself or someone else.

What Nurses Know...

Normal anxiety is sporadic and based on certain situations, such as a big exam. Anxiety disorders, including PTSD, tend to be chronic and interfere with many life functions. If your anxiety interferes with your daily routines, your relationships, or your job, it is no longer normal anxiety.

Just reading about all this anxiety is enough to make you anxious. If it does, take a break and put the book down.

Anxiety disorder is a term used for a group of disorders characterized by intense and/or persistent anxiety. These disorders include PTSD, and also generalized anxiety disorder (GAD), social anxiety disorder (also called social phobia), specific phobia, panic disorder with and without agoraphobia, obsessive-compulsive disorder (OCD), anxiety secondary to a medical condition, acute stress disorder (ASD), and substance-induced anxiety disorder, all of which will be explained later in this chapter. Anxiety disorders are one of the most common psychiatric illnesses affecting children and adults. An estimated 40 million American adults suffer from anxiety disorders, and

What Nurses Know...

The Anxiety Disorders Association of America (ADAA) is the leader in advocacy, education, training, and research for anxiety and stress-related disorders. Visit their website for more information on anxiety and anxiety disorders (www.adaa.org).

only about one-third of them receive treatment, even though these disorders are highly treatable.

The differences between anxiety and anxiety disorder primarily focus on time and intensity. Anxiety is brief and fleeting; anxiety disorders are lasting. Anxiety is being nervous about riding in elevators but getting on anyway, while anxiety disorder means avoiding the elevator completely, even if it means climbing ten flights of stairs. Anxiety is being worried about getting the flu and using hand sanitizer; anxiety disorder is being worried about germs in general and washing ones hands so frequently that it causes bleeding. Anxiety is being exposed to trauma and having some nightmares about it; anxiety disorder is being exposed to trauma and still having flashbacks years later, as with PTSD.

ACUTE STRESS DISORDER

Acute stress disorder (ASD) develops within the first month after a severe trauma. Symptoms of ASD overlap those of PTSD, but the diagnosis of PTSD cannot be given until the symptoms last for a month or more. Persons with ASD are also more likely to experience feeling as if they are outside of their bodies or feeling as if they do not know where they are.

Like PTSD, the impact of trauma is influenced by several factors, particularly: the severity of the event; the duration of the event; the proximity to the event (whether the event was directly experienced or witnessed); the type of the event; and the intent (whether the event was planned or accidental). Human acts of violence, especially those that are particularly cruel, create a greater risk for this disorder than natural events. Individuals with ASD develop dissociative responses (the mind distances itself from experiences, usually due to trauma) and may experience decreased emotional responsiveness, often finding it difficult to experience pleasure and frequently feeling guilty. Symptoms appear during or immediately after the trauma, last for at least two days, and resolve within four weeks after the con-clusion of the traumatic event or when the diagnosis is changed. Symptoms lasting more than four weeks may warrant a diagno-sis of PTSD, provided the full criteria for that disorder are met.

The criteria for a diagnosis of ASD are:

1. Exposure to a traumatic event in which the person experi-enced or witnessed an actual or threatened death or serious injury and the person's response involved intense fear, help-lessness, or horror.
2. The person has three or more of the following symptoms: a sense of numbing, detachment, or absence of emotional responsiveness; a reduction in awareness of his or her sur-roundings, feeling as if the world seems unreal as if in a dream or movie (derealization), or feeling as if he or she is out f his or her own body; or dissociative amnesia (unable to remember personal events (depersonalization).
3. Persistent re-experiencing of the traumatic event in at least one of the following ways: recurrent images, thoughts, dreams, or illusions, flashbacks, a sense of reliving the expe-rience, or distress on exposure to reminders of the traumatic event.
4. Avoidance of anything that causes recollections of the trauma.

What Nurses Know...

When women miscarry a pregnancy and suffer complicated bereavement, their healthcare providers may not consider the diagnosis of acute stress disorder or PTSD. If your PTSD symptoms started after losing a pregnancy, talk to your healthcare provider.

5. Severe symptoms of anxiety or increased arousal, such as difficulty sleeping, poor concentration, hypervigilance, or exaggerated startle response.

6. Impairment in social, occupational, or other important areas of functioning.

BRIEF PSYCHOTIC DISORDER

A brief psychotic disorder is an uncommon illness that lasts from one day to one month. Symptoms include: delusions, hallucinations, disorganized speech, and grossly disorganized or catatonic behavior. Other possible expressions are a rapidly changing mood, disorientation, impaired attention, outlandish dress or behavior, screaming or muteness, and impaired memory for recent events.

The cause of this disorder is unknown. Some studies have supported a genetic vulnerability to brief psychotic disorder. However, one or more severe stress factors, such as traumatic events, family conflict, employment problems, severe illness, death of a loved one, and uncertain immigration status, can precipitate the disorder.

ADJUSTMENT DISORDER

Adjustment disorder is a greater behavioral and emotional reaction to a particular life stress than would normally be expected. Like PTSD and ASD, adjustment disorder requires a precipitating stressor; however, unlike the other two disorders, the stressor in adjustment disorder can be of any severity. Thus, adjustment disorder may develop from common negative events such as marital conflict, financial problems, work or school problems, sexuality issues, and even life transitions such as adolescence and midlife. The stressor may be a single event (relationship break-up), multiple events (failing grades), recurrent (business failures), continuous (living in a dangerous neighborhood), or even positive (getting married).

Adjustment disorder can involve a wide range of symptoms. The person may experience a depressed mood with tearfulness and feelings of hopelessness, anxiety, and worry, or a combination of these symptoms. Some persons experience conduct disturbances and engage in acts that violate the rights of others, such as vandalism, reckless driving, or fighting. By definition, adjustment disorders last no longer than six months, unless they are reactions to chronic stressors.

OBSESSIVE-COMPULSIVE DISORDER

Obsessive-compulsive disorder (OCD) causes recurrent intrusive thoughts, but these thoughts are not related to a traumatic event and are experienced as inappropriate. These recurrent and unwelcome thoughts (obsessions) may be accompanied by repetitive behaviors (compulsions), such as checking and re-checking, counting, or hand washing. These rituals provide only temporary relief from the intrusive thoughts, and thus the cycle of obsessions and compulsions persists.

STOCKHOLM SYNDROME

Stockholm Syndrome is a psychological state where victims identify with their offenders. The term was originally used in cases of kidnapping and hostage situations, but has been extended to other forms of violence, including intimate partner

What Nurses Know...

Adjustment disorder may follow a common life stress, such as a relationship break-up, and rarely lasts longer than six months. PTSD occurs after a significant stress, such as a life-threatening event, and lasts longer.

violence and child abuse. There is no universally accepted definition of Stockholm syndrome, but it has been suggested that
it is present if one or more of the following is observed: positive
feelings by the captive person toward the captor; negative feelings by the captive person toward the police or authorities trying to win his or her release; and positive feelings by the captor
toward his or her captive. The following conditions must be met
for Stockholm syndrome to occur: a perceived threat to survival
and a belief that the captor is willing to carry out that threat;
a perception by the captive of some small kindness from the
captor within the context of terror; isolation from perspectives
other than those of the captor; and perceived inability to escape.
One study examined how aspects of Stockholm syndrome were
identified in the responses of adult survivors of child sexual
abuse, and appeared to impact on their ability to criminally
report offenders.

In general, PTSD results from trauma. Therefore, the symptoms of PTSD must occur after the traumatic event, not before.
If symptoms such as avoidance, numbing, and increased arousal
were present before the traumatic event, another disorder, such
as major depression or a different anxiety disorder, may be
present.

Why Me? Understanding How You Developed PTSD

"I and my sisters were digitally raped and otherwise molested (I'm sure you can imagine what I mean) for years by my father on an almost-daily basis. He would literally go from bed to bed. Christmas morning was the one day of the year that he left us alone. He could strike fear in our hearts with a simple glare. I had an emotional breakdown over the ongoing abuse at the age of 21; my mother refused to believe me even after my father confessed and went into therapy. Finally, my mother stated coldly, "This is over; your father is cured. It will never be discussed again." Like a fool, I believed her. I really thought it was over." ABBY

You may know the exact moment that triggered your PTSD because it plays over and over again in your mind, but you may not know why that moment refuses to leave your memory. Many people suffer from traumas, but they don't all develop PTSD. So you probably ask yourself, "Why me?"

Heroes face a problem or challenge and, once presented with this problem, can no longer remain in the comfort of their original world. Trauma knocked you out of your original world, which may or may not have been a nice place, and that trauma has become a steadfast villain in your life. Before you can eradicate that villain, you need to know everything you can about him. Just how did that villain trauma cause you to develop PTSD?

A Perfect Storm: The Causes of PTSD

Researchers are still working to understand the causes of PTSD. Most mental health disorder are caused by a mix of things, and PTSD is probably no different. Thus, PTSD is most likely a combination of four factors: your brain and your body's response to stress; genetics, particularly a predisposition to anxiety and depression; your personality; and your environment and life experience, including traumas since childhood.

What Nurses Know . . .

Reminder: *PTSD typically occurs after an individual experiences or witnesses severe trauma. The trauma may be a violent personal assault, war, natural disaster, severe accident, or the diagnosis of a life-threatening disease. The person first responds with intense fear, helplessness, or horror, and later develops a response to the event that is characterized by persistently re-experiencing the event, with resultant symptoms of numbness, avoidance, and hyperarousal.*

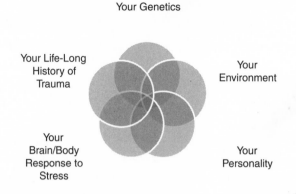

Your Genetics

Your Life-Long
History of
Trauma

Your
Environment

Your
Brain/Body
Response to
Stress

Your
Personality

Figure 2.1 Combined Causes of PTSD

YOUR BRAIN/BODY RESPONSE TO STRESS

Humans are hard wired to react to stress. A threat to our lives or personal integrity triggers an automatic response known as the "fight-or-flight" response, which dates back to our caveman ancestors. Seconds after the threat, our bodies release a cascade of hormones and brain chemicals (called neurotransmitters) that run through the body and mobilize every cell into action. Two major stress responses create the fight-or-flight response.

The first response to a stressor is the release of norepinephrine (also called noradrenaline) from the brainstem. This activates the adrenal glands to release epinephrine (also called adrenaline) and increases sympathetic nervous system tone. This increased tone results in an increased heart rate, higher blood pressure, and an increased breathing rate, as well as decreased digestive activity.

The second response comes from the hypothalamic–pituitary–adrenal axis. Stress stimulates release of a series of hormones that eventually result in the release of cortisol, the primary stress hormone. Cortisol increases sugar (glucose) in the

What Nurses Know...

The "fight-or-flight" response is the body's reaction to perceived threat or danger. The body releases specific hormones that speed the heart rate, slow digestion, push blood flow to major muscle groups, and change various other nervous system functions to give the body a burst of energy and strength. This burst of energy allowed cavemen to either fight or run away when threatened with danger, and allows modern man to do the same and deal with contemporary stressors. This brain/body function system is also designed to return the body to normal after the stressor disappears.

blood-stream so it can go to skeletal muscles, increasing your ability to fight or run away. Cortisol augments the adrenaline-related increases in heart rate and blood pressure, decreases functions that are nonessential to the fight-or-flight response, including digestion, and creates cognitive effects that limit memory processing during a highly stressful event. Once the immediate danger disappears, the body begins to shut down the stress response.

The "fight-or-flight" response is normal, healthy, and adaptive. It helps keep us safe. However, when it occurs too frequently or is greatly prolonged, you begin to experience the negative effects of stress. If your body does not shut down the fight-or-flight or stress reaction, you can continue to feel stress effects. A combination of higher-than-normal arousal hormone levels and lower-than-normal calming hormone levels may create the conditions for PTSD. When you have PTSD, you may also live in a constant state of fear and anxiety. You may not see the world

What Nurses Know...

● ●

The fight-or-flight response is supposed to allow our bodies to return to normal after the perceived threat disappears. However, in today's time of chronic stress, this may not happen when or as often as it should, and chronic stress results, which can result in damage to the body, mind, and spirit.

as a safe place. Instead, you may see danger everywhere, especially in places that remind you of the trauma.

The amygdala, a tiny but complicated almond-shaped mass in the brain, alerts the body to danger and activates hormonal systems. The amygdala is involved with how we learn about fear. There is some evidence that this structure is hyperactive in people with PTSD, creating a type of "false alarm" response. Research has shown that exposure to traumatic stimuli can lead to fear conditioning, with resultant activation of the amygdala and associated structures, including the hypothalamus, which links the nervous system and endocrine system. This activation and its accompanying brain chemical and hormone activities produce many of the symptoms of PTSD.

The hippocampus (one of the first regions of the brain to suffer damage in Alzheimer's disease) plays an important role in the formation of memory. Some evidence shows that people with PTSD have a loss of volume in this structure, which may account for some of the memory deficits and other symptoms in PTSD. Other research shows that neurochemicals may be involved in PTSD: A hormonal system known as the hypothalamic-pituitary-adrenal axis becomes disrupted in people with PTSD. The hypothalamic-pituitary-adrenal axis is involved in

What Nurses Know...

Persons with PTSD have abnormal levels of stress hormones that cause them to essentially live in constant "fight-or-flight" mode, making stress management all the more important.

normal stress reactions, and its disruption in people with PTSD can again be seen as a kind of "false alarm." Medication may act to reverse neurochemical dysfunction in PTSD in a manner that switches off the false alarms. It may even be possible to predict the development of PTSD based on the early psychological and neurochemical changes in people who have been exposed to a traumatic event.

YOUR GENETICS

Family members of individuals with PTSD may have a higher prevalence of PTSD than similarly trauma-exposed family members who did not develop PTSD. This has been found in trauma-exposed adult children of Holocaust survivors. Adult children of survivors with PTSD were more likely to develop PTSD following trauma exposure than were adult children of survivors without PTSD. This pattern has also been found in Cambodian refugees. However, family members frequently share experiences, and thus family studies cannot tell whether a disorder runs in families due to genetic or environmental reasons. In other words, we still are not sure whether this is nature or nurture.

Twin studies have made three important contributions to understanding the genetic component of PTSD. First and probably foremost, genetic factors influence how we react and respond to exposure to potentially traumatic events. Second,

What Nurses Know...

Genetic factors may influence the relationship between a person's exposure to trauma and that person's likelihood of developing PTSD.

twin studies suggest genetic influences explain a large proportion of vulnerability to PTSD even after accounting for genetic influences on potentially traumatic event exposure. Third, twin studies of PTSD indicate some degree of distinctness of genetic influences on PTSD, as well as some degree of overlap in genetic contributions with other mental disorders. Genetic influences on major depression account for the majority of the genetic variance in PTSD. Genetic influences common to generalized anxiety disorder and panic disorder symptoms account for genetic variance in PTSD, as do those common to alcohol, drug, and nicotine dependence. Therefore, the majority of genes that affect risk for PTSD also influence risk for other psychiatric disorders and vice versa. However, the twin studies cannot tell us which genes are important in PTSD etiology.

Recently, a team of researchers from the Emory University School of Medicine and the University of Vermont found that abnormal blood levels of a hormone called PACAP (pituitary adenylate cyclase-activating polypeptide), which is produced in response to stress, is strongly linked to PTSD in women. In many animals, PACAP modulates central nervous system activity, metabolism, blood pressure, pain sensitivity, and the immune function. However, its role in human fear and anxiety is little understood. This new research shows that women (but not men) with high blood levels of PACAP display more of the symptoms of PTSD, including difficulty discriminating between fear and safety signals and being easier to startle. In one group of people, most of whom had experienced significant trauma, the women with above-average PACAP levels had PTSD symptom scores five times higher than those of women with lower-than-average PACAP levels. This study shows promise for developing blood and genetic tests to identify persons who have PTSD and for developing tools to predict whether a patient is going to be susceptible to PTSD.

Children may show signs of PTSD because they are upset by their parent's PTSD symptoms. This is called secondary traumatization. Trauma and symptoms can also be passed from parent to child or between generations. Called intergenerational transmission of trauma, this been seen in the families of Holocaust survivors and families of combat veterans with PTSD. In some cases, when a family teaches their child not to talk about disturbing events, thoughts, or feelings, the child's anxiety gets worse. The child may worry about causing the parent's symptoms if the child talks about the trauma, and may create his or her own ideas about what happened to the parent. This can be worse than what actually happened. Other parents share too many details about the events, and their children may experience PTSD symptoms in response to these terrible images.

What Nurses Know ...

Some victims of intergenerational trauma, including Native Americans who, like families of Holocaust victims, are survivors of genocide, may have a higher trauma threshold due to severe chronic trauma and may not exactly fit the PTSD criteria. If you are a victim of intergenerational trauma and think your symptoms are too mild to be classified as PTSD, tell your healthcare provider about your history and its impact on symptom minimization.

Children may share in their parent's symptoms as a way to connect with the parent, or they may also re-enact some aspect of the trauma because they see that their parent has difficulty separating the past trauma from the present moment. This may be happening in your family – another strong reason why you need to continue your journey to recovery and move on with the rest of your life.

YOUR PERSONALITY

Several researchers have looked at personality factors related to PTSD, including emotions, reaction to higher levels of general stress, and ineffective coping mechanisms.

The key emotions currently associated with PTSD are fear, helplessness, and horror; however, research has shown that other emotions also play a role in PTSD. Some researchers found that persons with PTSD display a range of emotions that include anger, sadness, and shame others found that shame in victims of violent crime has been shown to predict PTSD symptoms after trauma. Some people suffer memory loss after the trauma, especially those who sustained head injury and those who were victims of drug-related rape. This makes it difficult for them to recall specific emotions that may have been experienced due to the traumatic event. Some traumatic events, including car accidents, happen so fast that it is difficult for an individual to be aware of the emotional state at the time.

What Nurses Know...

Your temperament and coping abilities help determine your reaction to stress. There is a huge difference between telling yourself "I can deal with this" and "I can't handle this." Your perspective can easily become a self-fulfilling prophecy.

Some people respond to trauma by feeling numb or dazed, which can impact their ability to register or fully experience their emotional states at the time of the trauma. This dissociation is a specific type of response to a stressful experience where the person can feel separated or cut-off from him- or herself and/or the surroundings. Persons who are in a "dissociative state" may feel numb, may lose track of time, feel as though they are floating outside of their bodies, or have no memories about a certain period of time.

Researchers have also made a distinction between primary emotions, those experienced at the time of the trauma, and secondary emotions, those experienced after a traumatic event. These secondary emotions may be different from primary emotions because they are based on cognitive appraisals following the trauma. These researchers suggest that these secondary emotional reactions are likely to have an impact on the later development of PTSD.

Higher levels of general stress can place a person at increased risk for developing PTSD. Chronic stress can take a toll on anyone and can weaken a person's defenses against trauma-induced stress in the same way that hardship can weaken the immune system. Persons impacted by the trauma of child abuse, domestic violence, or war are usually already experiencing chronic stress related to that trauma. Other events that are not of traumatic magnitude but that are still stressful, such as divorce, job loss, and financial problems, can also weaken an individual's defenses.

Stressful living, inexperience dealing with stressful situations and other factors can result in persons having ineffective coping mechanisms. This can predispose them to PTSD because they are totally unprepared to handle traumatic stress. Individuals may cope by avoiding other people, including their family and friends. Avoidance leads to feelings of isolation, making the person feel like he or she is facing life all alone. When this happens, problems seem to magnify, along with negative thoughts and feelings of sadness and fear. Coping with anger can also cause people to distance

What Nurses Know...

Inadequate coping can precipitate PTSD. It can also aggravate PTSD symptoms because you need healthy coping skills to deal with both your internal triggers (emotions, memories, and bodily sensations) and external triggers (people, places, and situations).

themselves from others, even if that distance is not wanted. While it is natural to feel angry after trauma, continuously losing one's temper and acting out adds to the problems and makes it more difficult to recover from the traumatic event. Others deal with traumatic stress by turning to substances - alcohol or other drugs - to escape their problems. This results in the person being predisposed to two problems, PTSD and substance abuse.

YOUR ENVIRONMENT

Your environment plays a critical role on your mental health in general. Obviously, people who live in severely dysfunctional

What Nurses Know...

A nonsupportive environment can lead to PTSD or worsen it. If your family is not supportive, find support elsewhere. To find a PTSD support group near you, talk to your healthcare provider, therapist, or clergy person; check your phone book and contact your local mental health services or check with the National Center for PTSD at www.ptsd.va.gov or (802) 296-6300.

homes or those who spend months on the battlefield live in environments filled with stress. However, negative environments can be subtle. Lack of social support from family and the community plays a role in the development of PTSD. This can be especially true of sexual assault victims who are not believed or who are blamed for the assault. These problems can arise from the family, but can also come from the community in the forms of the criminal justice and healthcare systems when the victim seeks justice or care for injuries.

Trauma and PTSD

In general, exposure to traumatic events is the rule, not the exception, for most people. The lifetime prevalence of exposure to any trauma increases to nearly 90% when broader criteria are employed, with more than half of individuals with trauma exposure reporting exposure to more than one event. The diagnosis of PTSD warrants that the individual experienced a trauma. In fact, the first diagnostic criterion for PTSD requires exposure to a traumatic event in which:

1. The person experienced, witnessed, or was confronted with an event(s) that involved actual or threatened death, serious injury, or a threat to the physical integrity.
2. The person's response involved intense fear, helplessness, or horror.

However, as noted earlier in this chapter, trauma alone is inadequate for the development of PTSD. There needs to be a mix of factors, as well as specific conditions related to the trauma.

Trauma is more likely to negatively affect a person who disconnects (dissociates), feels alone, and isolated, and believes that that he or she is somehow responsible for the traumatic event. These beliefs and feelings create artificial separation from others and unnecessary shame regarding the event. Certain aspects of the trauma also impact on the development of PTSD, and these aspects can increase the risk of developing PTSD when alone or in combination with each other:

- *Severity of the trauma:* Personal vulnerabilities weigh more heavily on the development of PTSD when the traumatic event is considered a low-level stress or trauma, such as a romantic break-up. On the other hand, more severe trauma, such as sexual assault, tends to lead to PTSD more often and result in more chronic stress.
- *Proximity of the trauma*: The person's proximity to the traumatic event is directly related to that person's degree of distress and potential to develop PTSD. For example, those who are closest to a mass shooting tend to report higher levels of stress, as well as the incidence and severity of PTSD, than those located farther away from the incident.
- *Type of the trauma*: The type of trauma interacts with other factors, such as age, gender, and trauma severity, to reveal different PTSD susceptibilities. Studies have shown that the risk of PTSD varied with these stressors: rape (49%), physical assault (32%), other sexual assault (24%), serious accident or injury (17%), shooting/stabbing (15%), unexpected death of relative or friend (14%), life-threatening illness of a child (10%), witnessing of a killing or serious injury (7%), and natural disaster (4%).
- *Nature of the trauma*: The risk for developing PTSD increases if the trauma is sudden, unpredicted, enduring, or recurring. The risk also rises if the event poses a real threat of harm to the victim, if the trauma is multidimensional (hurricane disaster followed by floods, home invasion, and rape), and if the trauma occurs early in life.
- *Perception of the trauma*: Perception is critical and related to personality: If the person perceives that the trauma is severe, then the trauma is severe for that person.

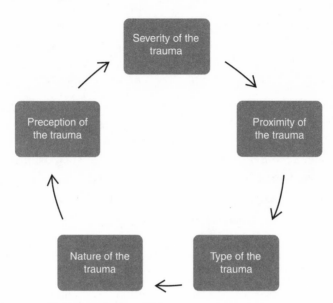

Figure 2.2 Characteristics of Trauma

TYPES OF TRAUMA

According to the National Center for PTSD, approximately 60% of men and 50% of women experience at least one traumatic event during their lives. Of those who experience trauma, about 8% of men and 20% of women will develop PTSD. For some events, however, such as combat and sexual assault, a greater percentage of people develop PTSD.

War

PTSD, once called "shell shock" or battle fatigue, was first brought to public attention by war veterans. During and after a war, there is an increased number of veterans or active duty military personnel returning from the war, as well as family members who have lost a loved one or whose loved one is missing in action (MIA) or has been taken prisoner of war (POW). There may be increased distress in veterans of other wars, conflicts, and peacekeeping missions. All of these people may be experiencing symptoms of PTSD. The wars in Iraq and Afghanistan have caused increased rates of PTSD among soldiers, particularly female soldiers (although female soldiers are more likely to seek help), and the additional risk from the unprecedented rates of multiple deployments.

According to the National Center for PTSD, combat troops face a number of stressors during war, and these stressors place them on alert around the clock. They are at risk of death or injury; they may see others hurt or killed; and they themselves may have to kill or wound others. For many, being deployed for long periods of time can cause problems at home or work. This can be more stressful for National Guard and Reserve troops who had not expected to be away for long. An additional stressor is military sexual trauma (MST), which refers to sexual assault or repeated, threatening sexual harassment that occurs in the military. MST can happen to men and women, and it can occur during peace time, training, or war.

Violent Victimization

A violent crime may only last seconds, but its effects can be significant and last a lifetime. Victims may suffer physical, psychological, social, and/or financial trauma that can leave them devastated if they do not get proper intervention. Numerous studies have examined the long-term consequences of relationship violence during childhood. These studies have suggested that physical and sexual abuse in early life can lead to problems in adulthood, including poor mental and physical health, as well as higher rates of substance abuse. However, only a few studies have examined the long-term consequences of relationship violence in adulthood. They have suggested that women who experience relationship violence in adulthood have poor health trajectories, including depressive symptoms, functional impairment, and high alcohol consumption. One study showed that past-year abuse was independently associated with increased hospital admissions and that psychological effects of recent abuse combined with depression may increase the rates of medical/surgical hospitalizations. Victims may fear for their lives, and in some cases, especially those of intimate partner violence, victims may be in danger of being killed. Past offenders may not yet have been caught or may be out on bail or on probation or parole.

Many victims lose their jobs because of absenteeism due to injury or illness related to the violence. Absences can also occur from court appearances. Victims of intimate partner violence and stalking may have to move many times to avoid violence. This is costly and can interfere with continuity of employment. Victims may also have had to forego financial security during divorce proceedings to avoid further abuse, and many become impoverished as they grow older.

Several factors influence a victim's response to, and recovery from, sexual assault: age and developmental maturity of the victim; frequency, severity, and duration of the assault(s); setting of the attack; level of violence and injury inflicted; response by the criminal justice system; community attitudes and values; the victim's relationship to the offender; meaning attributed to the traumatic event by the sexual assault survivor; response to the attack by police, medical personnel, and victim advocates; response to the attack by the victim's loved ones; and the social

What Nurses Know...

Criminal victimization is unpredictable and often unexpected. It is debilitating and demoralizing, and its effects can be long-term and difficult to overcome. Victims suffer physically, emotionally, psychologically, and financially from their victimization, and they are often burdened by the intricacies of the criminal justice system.

support network available to the victim. Some sexual assault survivors find that they can recover relatively quickly, while others feel the lasting effects of their victimization throughout their lifetimes.

Criminal victimization is a frightening and unsettling experience. Reactions to victimization vary. If your PTSD resulted from victimization, you may still feel one or more of the following emotions:

- *Shock, disbelief, and denial:* Victims may find it hard to believe they have been victimized and may even pretend it didn't happen. Denial may be present for months and even years. Once the shock fades away, other emotions kick in, such as anger, fear, frustration, confusion, guilt, shame, and grief.
- *Anger or rage:* Victims may be angry with the offender, family, friends, the criminal justice system or other service providers, God, or even themselves. Hate is not uncommon, and many victims have strong desire for revenge or getting even. Because the rest of society does not approve of these emotions, they can leave the victim feeling like an outcast. However, victims are certainly justified to feel anger toward the person or people who harmed them. Anger can be compounded when the offender is not charged or convicted and the victim therefore does not get justice.
- *Fear or terror:* Victims commonly feel terror or fear following a crime that involved a threat to their safety or life. This fear can last for a long time, and under certain circumstances, can become debilitating.
- *Frustration:* Many victims are frustrated if they cannot access the support and information necessary for their healing, including the support needed from the criminal justice system.
- *Powerlessness or helplessness:* Many victims feel helplessness or powerlessness when a crime occurs, especially if they were unable to fend off, offender, call for help, or run away.

- *Confusion*: Victims may become confused if they are unsure of what actually happened -- crimes often occur quickly and are chaotic. Victims can also become confused while searching for answers to unanswerable questions such as "Why did this happen to me?"
- *Guilt*: Many victims feel guilty for not doing more to prevent what happened. Some victims experience "survivor guilt," feeling guilty that they survived while someone else was injured or even killed.
- *Shame and humiliation*: Some victims blame themselves, especially victims of sexual abuse or assault or domestic violence. Sex offenders often degrade the victim by making the victim do humiliating things. Victims of sexual assault have long-lasting feelings of "being dirty" that cannot be "washed away." Some victims even feel self-hatred because they believe that they can no longer be loved by their loved ones.
- *Grief or sorrow*: Sadness is frequently the most powerful long-term reaction to crime, and it is common for victims to become depressed.

What Nurses Know...

Crime victims have three basic needs immediately following a crime: the need to feel safe; the need to express their emotions; and the need to know what happens next. If you were victimized and these needs were not met at that time, contact your local Victims Resource Center. If your victimization was recent and you still feel unsafe, the Center may be able to help you obtain an order of protection. They may also be able to help you with other needs, such as financial compensation for the crime.

- *Revictimization*: The inappropriate treatment of rude, apathetic, or just plain incompetent criminal justice and healthcare professionals often causes victims to feel that they have been revictimized.

Natural Disasters

Millions of people experience natural disasters every year—earthquakes, floods, hurricanes, tornados, tsunamis, and fires. Disasters cause death, physical injury, and loss of home, possessions, and community. Some survivors suffer significant distress and psychiatric disorders, and many report non-specific distress, health problems, chronic problems in living, and resource loss. The most common condition was PTSD, followed by depression, and then other anxiety disorders. Risk factors for problems included more severe exposure, being female, being middle age, belonging to an ethnic minority group, having prior psychiatric problems, and having weak or deteriorating psychosocial resources. Other factors that place people at risk for poor recovery after a natural disaster include: not functioning well before the disaster; having no experience dealing with disasters; dealing with other stressors after the disaster; poor self-esteem; thinking that they are uncared for by others or that they have little control over what happens to them; lacking the capacity to manage stress; the death of someone close; injury to self or another family member; life threat; panic, horror, or similar feelings during the disaster; being separated from family; great property loss; and being forced to leave home.

Most people improve as time passes. Lasting symptoms are likely when people experienced other forms of life stress in addition to the disaster or had poor self-esteem or weak social ties. For example, long after Hurricane Andrew, people felt less positive about the quality of their social relationships than they had felt before the disaster, which suggests that perceptions of social support are also harmed by disaster experience.

Accidents

Accidents are one of the leading causes of death and injury in the United States, but while many people experience some type of accident during their lifetimes, most do not develop PTSD. Accident severity, fatalities, and severe injuries contribute to the potential for development of PTSD. People who perceived a significant threat to their lives, regardless of the extent of their injuries, are at risk, and horrific and intrusive memories immediately following a motor vehicle accident are a strong predictor of PTSD symptoms, regardless of the severity of the accident. Another factor associated with symptom persistence is litigation. This can be problematic because those pursuing legal action may be more severely injured, and the length of legal battles can be considerable.

Survivors of motor vehicle accidents often face traumatic stress. As with the other conditions already described, there are specific factors that place people more at risk for PTSD following a motor vehicle accident. These are broken down into three categories, pre-accident, accident-related, and post-accident factors, all of which are similar in other traumas related to PTSD. Pre-accident factors include poor coping skills prior to the accident, the presence of a pre-accident mental health problem such as depression, and poor social support. Accident-related factors are potential threat to life, seriousness of injury, fear of dying,

What Nurses Know...

Long-term emotional consequences of disaster strongly relate to the survivor's thoughts or beliefs. People at risk for mental health problems, including PTSD, think that they are uncared for by others, have little control over what happens to them, or lack the capacity to manage stress.

and loss of significant others. Post-accident factors are the rate of physical recovery from injury, the level of social support from friends and family, and the level of active reengagement in both work and social activities.

Terrorism

The events of September 11, 2001, left more than 3,500 people dead or injured; tens of thousands of people knew someone who was killed or injured, and millions witnessed the attack through the media. People at all levels were affected: victims, victims' families and friends, police, fire fighters, rescue workers, emergency medical personnel, mental-health providers, witnesses to the event, volunteers, members of the media, and people around the world.

Terrorism eats away at both the individual's and the community's sense of security and safety; it challenges the basic need of humans to see the world as predictable, orderly, and controllable.

Terrorist acts create feelings of injustice that lead to anger, frustration, helplessness, fear, and a desire for revenge. However, the mechanisms for recovery from traumatic events are strong and trauma experts agree that the psychological outcome of communities as a whole will be resilience, not psychopathology. For most people, fear, anxiety, reexperiencing the event, urges to avoid event reminders, and hyperarousal symptoms will gradually decrease over time. Those most likely to develop PTSD are those who experience the greatest magnitude of exposure to the traumatic event, such as victims and their families, and sometimes rescue workers.

Torture

The United Nations defines torture as the deliberate infliction of severe emotional or physical pain or suffering, usually through cruel, inhumane, or degrading treatment or punishment. Intentional torture can be more emotionally damaging than other forms of trauma, including war and sexual assault, and may even accompany these other traumas. PTSD among torture survivors is about 36%, a much higher incidence than other trauma. Victims of torture may also develop depression, somatization (physical symptoms from psychological stress), obsessive-compulsive symptoms, anger, hostility, phobias, paranoid ideas, and psychotic episodes.

Other Possible Traumas

Research has shown that there are many other types of traumas that can result in PTSD:

- PTSD can develop from multiple but less severe traumas ("microtraumas"), which can be a consequence of a history of longstanding emotional neglect, humiliation, or inaccurate attribution of blame. These non-life-threatening emotional traumas occur more frequently and are often more psychologically harmful than a single catastrophic event.
- Late-life spousal bereavement is sometimes associated with psychological problems, usually depression. However, results from a Danish study suggested that late-life spousal bereavement results in PTSD with equal frequency as general samples of bereaved persons. The study also found that the prevalence of PTSD in the first months after bereavement was more elevated than the level of depression.
- While the incidence of PTSD after a heart attack (myocardial infarction) was low, a small percent of patients developed "subsyndromal" PTSD, meaning they did not exhibit all the characteristic symptoms. The emotional status of the patients at the time of the heart attack and the person's reaction to the event were important factors in the development of PTSD symptoms. Blacks and younger patients were found to have increased risk of developing PTSD symptoms post-heart attack.

- People with cancer are considered to be at risk for PTSD. The physical and emotional shock of having a life-threatening disease, experiencing the side effects of treatment, and living with repeated threats to one's body and life are traumatic experiences for many cancer patients.
- Traumatic brain injury occurs from a sudden blow or jolt to the head, often during some type of trauma, such as an accident, blast or explosion, or a fall. Traumatic brain injury, including concussion, has been associated with subsequent PTSD in survivors of terrorist attacks and war injuries.

As you can see, although your PTSD was triggered by a trauma, it was still probably caused by a combination of factors. Hopefully, this knowledge will better enable you to understand why you developed PTSD and relieve you of any guilt you may feel in thinking you brought this upon yourself. Your PTSD developed because of a perfect storm of factors that collided at the time you experienced that traumatic event.

You've come a long way on your hero's journey already. You are armed with knowledge about your disorder, and you know about the villainous trauma. Now you are ready to tackle the villain's henchmen – the symptoms of PTSD.

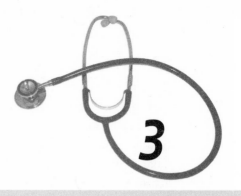

Symptoms: When Every Day Is Yesterday

"I'm on the stairs trying to get to the phone, when he grabs my arm. It's been years since the police dragged my husband from the house, but somehow I keep going back, as if I slip into some nightmarish time warp. And here it is today, he's long gone, and I'm still afraid that I won't be able to get to the phone for help." VERONICA

As a trauma survivor, you instinctively used self-protective coping strategies to shield yourself from psychological harm at the time of the distressing experience. Today, however, those very same self-protective instincts now interfere with your life and hold you back on your journey. These symptoms can be frightening, debilitating, and overwhelming. Memories of the traumatic event may intrude on your waking hours, sleep time, or both, and impact your job, schooling, and relationships. You may find it difficult at times just to get through the day. But you can get those memories out of your life. To start kicking them out of the path of your journey, you first need to understand them.

PTSD symptoms generally begin within three months of the trauma; however, symptoms may be delayed as long as several months or years for some people, while others may experience acute traumatic stress syndrome and demonstrate symptoms soon after the event. Symptoms may wax and wane or even disappear completely. Symptoms may reactivate in response to reminders of the original trauma, new trauma, or even everyday events. Regardless of duration, symptoms tend to fall into three categories: persistent re-experiencing of the event, persistent avoidance of stimuli related to the event, and persistent symptoms of increased arousal. As you can see, persistence itself is a key factor of PTSD symptoms.

Re-Experiencing Symptoms

Intrusive symptoms are thoughts and memories that appear to happen in the here and now. They involve the traumatic event, which may in turn cause intense feelings of fear, helplessness, and horror similar to the feelings you had when the event actually happened.

There are many ways in which you may relive trauma, including spontaneous, upsetting memories, flashbacks, nightmares, and night terrors. The traumatic event may replay in your mind

What Nurses Know...

Re-experiencing symptoms *include: Recurrent distressing memories of the event, flashbacks, nightmares, might terrors, hallucinations, vivid feelings of the event happening again, physical reactions to triggers.*

unexpectedly without provocation. One study found that intrusions had a vivid perceptual content and were distressing, and appeared to be happening in the present.

FLASHBACKS

Memories sometimes feel so real that it's as if the trauma is actually happening again. When this happens, it's called a flashback. Also called "nowness," feelings that these sensations are coming from experiences in the present instead of memories from the past—and the emotions, physical reactions, and motor responses that accompany them—are the same as those experienced at the time of the original trauma. While experienced in flashbacks, this "nowness' may also be experienced through brief intrusive memories that do not involve loss of awareness of present surroundings. Flashbacks may be brief, where the person loses some connection with the present, or prolonged, where the person loses all awareness of the present and is transported back to the time of the trauma. Some people lose track of time during a flashback.

Flashbacks are a form of dissociation, a mental process that causes a lack of connection in your thoughts, memory, and sense of identity. Dissociation can be a normal mechanism that helps us block out horrifying experiences, such as having an "out

What Nurses Know ...

Flashbacks are memories of your traumatic event that intrude on the present, causing you to feel like you are back in the trauma. They usually appear as snippets of memories—the booming noise of the car crashing into the ravine, the stench of the rapist's breath, or the green skies of the tornado.

of body" experience when being sexually assaulted. Everyone experiences dissociation at one time or another. In its mild form, dissociation exists in the form of daydreaming, getting lost in a book, and driving down a familiar stretch of road and not remembering the last several miles.

Re-experiencing symptoms may be triggered by a variety of stimuli, including internal and external cues that include sights, sounds, smells, tastes, or bodily sensations such as pain, similar to stimuli present at the time of the trauma. A car back-fire may mimic an explosion and trigger memories for a combat veteran. News of a recent sexual or domestic assault or natural disaster may trigger a flashback. However, people with PTSD are often not aware of these triggers, and thus the intrusive memories appear to come out of the blue. The ease of triggering of re-experiencing memories may be linked to their persistence.

Researchers have found differences between people who had developed PTSD as a result of sexual assault or motor vehicle accident, and people who experienced sexual assault or a motor vehicle accident but did not develop PTSD. People with PTSD showed more activation in certain right-brain areas, while sub-jects without PTSD showed more activation in certain left-brain areas. The researchers suggested that this may help explain why people with PTSD tend to experience traumatic recall as sponta-neous visual flashbacks and why non-PTSD individuals are more apt to experience traumatic memories as verbal narratives.

Dealing with Flashbacks

Flashbacks can be frightening and debilitating. However, there are steps you can take to decrease or eradicate them.

- *Identify your triggers*: Flashbacks tend to be triggered by something that reminds you of the event: people, places, things, sounds. If you know your triggers, you can either limit your exposure to them or learn to cope with them. Your triggers are personal and sensual. Sights and sounds are the most common triggers, followed by touch, smell, and taste. Start a journal; write it in a notebook or type it into your laptop or tablet. Choose whatever method is most convenient and portable for you. After you experience a flashback, write down what you saw, heard, touched, smelled, and tasted prior to it. Write down everything, no matter how slight or insignificant it may seem. Even a seemingly pleasant sensation can be a trigger. For example, certain aftershaves may normally be appealing, but a specific one can become a noxious trigger if it had been worn by the person who assaulted you.

- *Recognize warning signs*: Your flashbacks may seem to come out of nowhere, but you most likely have signs that one is starting. You may begin to feel like you are slipping away or hovering over yourself. The room may start to look blurry. Use your journal. Try to identify those early feelings. If you can identify the beginning of a flashback, you can learn to stop it..

- *Get grounded*: Use your senses to bring yourself back to the present and to regain control.

  - *Sight*—Look around the room and name items out loud; turn on the news; read the newspaper; read your calendar; text, IM, or tweet a friend.

  - *Sound*—Listen to loud music; turn on the television; call a friend; talk out loud about current events.

  - *Touch*—Exercise; pet your dog or cat; spritz yourself with water; cuddle a stuffed animal; clap your hands; hold a piece of ice; go outside and experience the weather.

  - *Smell*—Smell something strong like peppermint, eucalyptus, sage, sandalwood, or basil.

  - *Taste* - Eat a lemon; drink strong bitter coffee; eat a hot pepper.

- *Talk to yourself*: Say: "This is just a flashback; it's not real." "I am in the here and now. It is [today's date], and I am in [your location]." "I am afraid, but I am not in any danger."

- *Get support*: Talk to a family member; call a friend, health-care provider, or therapist.

NIGHTMARES AND NIGHT TERRORS

Dreams are memories of mental activity that occur during sleep. People's accounts of the content of their dreams vary, based on the sleep stage from which they are awakened. Dreams experienced during REM (rapid eye movement) sleep tend to be strange and detailed with storyline plot associations, like trying to run away from something but getting nowhere. Dreams experienced in deep sleep are more diffuse, such as dreams about a color. The ability to remember dreams may reflect the dream's accessibility or distance from awake thought, with the highest recall

What Nurses Know . . .

Sleep consists of two basic stages: rapid eye movement (REM) and non-rapid eye movement (NREM). REM sleep is when most dreams occur. Dream recall can be vivid. NREM is made up of four stages with each lasting five to fifteen minutes:

I. *Light sleep*: Can be awakened without difficulty, but feel like you did not sleep. Thoughts drift.
II. *Preparation to enter deep sleep*: Still can be easily awakened but eyes will not see at first. May be able to vaguely recall dream if awakened.
III. *Deep sleep*: Takes loud sounds to awaken. Rarely able to remember thoughts.
IV. *Deepest sleep*: Very difficult to awaken. Very poor recall if awakened.

occurring during sleep stages that are most like those in the waking state.

Some professionals believe that dreams have no function, while others think that dreams are the nocturnal continuation of conscious thought or a reprogramming of the central nervous system for the next day's functioning. However, there is agreement that dreaming is important for learning and memory processing, and helping a person adapt to emotional and physical stress. Dreaming is good for you, but chronic nightmares and night terrors are not.

Trauma memories may haunt your dreams in the form of nightmares or night terrors. Nightmares are vivid and frightening episodes in which the dreamer suddenly awakens from sleep, usually during the REM phase of sleep. The dreamer can often describe the detailed dream plot and usually has trouble falling back to sleep.

About 5% of the general population complains of nightmares. Those who experience trauma tend to have more distressing and more frequent nightmares after the event, regardless of the type of trauma. People with PTSD are even more likely to have nightmares. For example, one study showed that 52% of Vietnam veterans with PTSD had nightmares fairly often, compared to 3% of civilians. Other studies found even higher rates of nightmares in persons with PTSD, as much as 71-96%.

Trauma nightmares often involve the same scary elements that were in the actual trauma. Survivors of robbery may have nightmares of being held at gun point, while survivors of hurricanes may dream of high winds and floods. Not all nightmares replay the event; however, people with PTSD are more likely to dream exact replays of a traumatic event than those without PTSD. People with PTSD generally report dreams in which they experience strong emotions, such as rage, intense fear, or grief that would have been appropriate reactions to the original traumatic event. Nightmares related to the trauma generally happen during REM sleep but can also occur at sleep onset, making falling asleep difficult. Sleep studies in these patients show that some people with PTSD have poor sleep maintenance, increased eye movement density, decreased percentage of REM sleep, and an increased tendency to have REM sleep at sleep onset.

Nightmares can result in sleep deprivation and thus can affect your health and well-being. Sleep deprivation can cause many medical problems, including heart disease, depression, and obesity. While the relationship is unclear, nightmares are also associated with suicide.

Night terrors are episodes of extreme terror and panic that usually occur early in the sleep period. They are associated with confusion and vocalizations, often a "blood-curdling" scream. People with night terrors are often difficult to arouse, and they have limited memory of their dream content.

Night terrors may last five to twenty minutes and occur during a phase of deep NREM (non-REM) sleep usually within an hour after the dreamer goes to bed (stage IV sleep). The dreamer is still asleep, although the eyes may be open. When the dreamer does wake up, he or she experiences a sense of fear or terror, accompanied by screaming, confusion, rapid heart rate, and an inability to explain what happened. Some people remember portions of the night terror, some the whole episode, and others have no recollection other than a sense of fear.

Dealing with Nightmares and Night Terrors

Nightmares and night terrors do not have to disrupt your life. You can learn to control them. Try some of these suggestions:

- Imagery rehearsal is a type of cognitive behavioral therapy for nightmares caused by PTSD. This technique can help you change your nightmares by rehearsing while you are awake how you would like them to be.
- Medications may be used in conjunction with therapy to treat PTSD-related nightmares; however, their efficacy has not been demonstrated as clearly as that of imagery

rehearsal treatment. One such medication is Minipress (generic name prazosin), which blocks some of the effects of adrenaline released in the body. When you have PTSD, your body may release too much adrenaline, a hormone that can make you feel stressed and cause nightmares. By helping to prevent you from having nightmares, Minipress may help you to sleep better, allowing you to feel healthier and more alert. This, in turn, may help lower your stress and help you feel more in control of your life. Like all medications, Minipress should be taken with caution. It is actually a high blood pressure medication, and thus may not be appropriate for you if your blood pressure tends to be low. Minipress lowers your blood pressure and can make you feel dizzy, so don't stand up too fast especially when first starting this medication and if the dosage is changed. This side effect should diminish with time. Other side effects include thinking and acting more slowly; lack of energy; slow heart rate (bradycardia); nausea; weakness; and coughing or wheezing, which means the airways that carry air to the lungs are narrowing (bronchospasm). Less common side effects are stuffy nose, headache, and swelling in the legs.

- Practice good sleep hygiene:
  - Go to bed at the same time each night.
  - Wake up at the same time each morning.
  - Avoid napping during the day.
  - Exercise regularly—but not just before bedtime.
  - Avoid long-term use of caffeine and other stimulants.
  - Avoid heavy or spicy foods prior to bedtime.
  - Avoid alcohol before bed.
  - Use comfortable bedding.
  - Set the room at a comfortable cool temperature.
  - Try relaxation exercises before going to bed (see Chapter 8).
  - Try a warm bath before bed.

What Nurses Know...

Cognitive-behavioral therapy (CBT) is a talk therapy that focuses on patterns of thinking that are maladaptive and the beliefs that underlie such thinking.

- Try drinking a glass of milk, herbal tea, or hot cocoa before bedtime.
- If you get cold hands and feet, keep them warm with socks and gloves.
- Leave your worries behind. Try using a "worry rock": Tell your worries to a small rock just before bedtime. When the rock becomes "full of worries," toss it away, symbolic of getting rid of your worries.
- Don't engage in stimulating activity before bed, go to bed too hungry or too full, or take over-the-counter sleeping pills or someone else's sleeping pills.

EMOTIONAL OR PHYSICAL REACTIONS

You may feel intensely distressing emotions or experience physical reactions when exposed to internal or external cues that symbolize or resemble an aspect of the traumatic event, such as the anniversary date of the event. Emotional responses include sadness, depression, and anxiety, while physical reactions include increased blood pressure and heart rate, rapid breathing, headache, muscle tension, nausea, and diarrhea, as well as general pain and low energy.

Emotions can have a snowball effect, and you may have emotional reactions in response to other emotions. For example, you may feel guilt because of anger toward your spouse for not protecting you from the trauma, even though your spouse was not there when it happened.

What Nurses Know...

Primary emotions *are those that we have as a first response to a situation or cue.* Secondary emotions *are emotional responses to primary emotions. Primary emotions tend to help, while secondary emotions tend to hinder.*

Emotions can be primary or secondary. Primary emotions occur as a direct result of experiencing some type of cue. For example, if your teenage daughter comes home after curfew, you may feel angry or irritated. These are primary emotions. If you feel fear after a flashback, this also is a primary emotion. Primary emotions are usually fast to emerge, occurring in close proximity to the cue. While sometimes upsetting, primary emotions are helpful because they inform us about our current situation and help us to act.

Secondary emotions, which are emotional responses to primary emotions, are less useful. Feeling fear after a flashback can be useful because it encourages you to learn how to manage those flashbacks. However, if you feel shame because of the fear, the shame can be more inhibiting than helpful. Secondary emotions last a long time and do not allow you to have valid, primary emotional reactions. People with PTSD may begin to connect the experience of certain emotions with traumatic memories or thoughts. For example, they may fear the experience of anxiety, which only increases the severity of the anxiety, potentially leading to unhealthy attempts to manage that emotion, such as alcohol or drug use.

Dealing with Emotional Reactions
Many people with PTSD have trouble regulating their emotions, and these mismanaged emotions lead to physical symptoms.

Fortunately, you can learn to better manage your emotions. Try some of these strategies:

- *Identify your emotions*: When you cannot identify your emotions, they can feel unpredictable and out of control, making it difficult for you to manage them. Pull out your journal, and begin a "My Emotions" chart. As you can see from the below example, the chart will help you identify your emotions, their triggers, their intensity, and how you manage them. The chart will help you identify the emotions that you need to work on— especially the secondary ones.
- *Increase positive emotions*: Not all emotions are bad. The chart will help you learn what makes you feel good. This way you can work on increasing those scenarios that result in positive emotions.

Cue	Emotion	Positive or Negative	Rate It on a Scale of 1 to 10	What You Did as a Result of the Emotion
Was in the electronic store at the mall and a news report about a rape came on the TV	Fear	Negative	8	Ran to the food mart and ate a large serving of ice cream
My 5-year-old broke the necklace that my grandmother gave me for my 13th birthday	Anger, guilt, happy	Negative to positive	3	I was angry but immediately felt guilty because I was angry at him. I scolded him for touching it without permission, but told him we could fix it. Then I felt good that I handled this well!

- *Use distractions*: Distractions can take your mind off your emotions, giving them time to decrease. When you feel a negative emotion rising, do something. Organize the kitchen junk drawer. Clean the refrigerator. Watch a sitcom or a cartoon. Take a walk. Do something that will occupy your time and mind so you don't focus on your emotions.

- *Write, draw, or paint your emotions*: Use your journal to write about how you feel. Not a writer? Try drawing or painting what you feel. Use some type of creative activity to override the negative emotions.

- *Use coping strategies*: Because you experience various emotions in reaction to various situations, you need an arsenal of coping strategies to deal with them. Passive and active coping strategies are examined in Chapter 8, but here are a few examples that you can use to deal with your emotions— the more that work for you, the greater your emotional management.

  - *Passive techniques*: Taking a long, warm bath; listening to soft music; yoga; aromatherapy (lavender, chamomile, sage, bergamot, frankincense, and sandalwood); blow bubbles; make a montage of your favorite photos; create a scrapbook; sew, knit or crochet; do your nails; play solitaire; play with a Slinky®; brush your hair; finish a crossword puzzle; pet the cat; or go to the movies.

  - *Active techniques*: Exercise; talking a walk; bang on a peg board; dance; swim; do a good deed; jump rope; play with the dog; play darts; jog around the park; or engage in a sport.

- *Volunteer*: One of the best ways to take your mind of your troubles is to help those less fortunate than you.

- *Use your support system*: Talk to your partner, friends, support group members, or therapist. Talking face-to-face over a soothing cup of herbal tea is best, but phone calls, instant messaging, web conferencing, and texting also work in today's tech times.

Dealing with Physical Reactions

The physical reactions from PTSD usually stem from emotional causes. This does not make them any less real, but it does mean that working on your emotions will most likely help your physical symptoms. However, do not take it for granted that all physical symptoms have psychological origins. Make sure you talk to your healthcare provider and have routine physical checkups to make sure you do not have any underlying physical illnesses.

PSYCHOTIC SYMPTOMS

PTSD may create psychotic symptoms in some people. Psychosis means loss of touch with reality. Symptoms are defined as either positive or negative. Positive psychotic symptoms refer to thoughts, perceptions, and behaviors that are ordinarily absent in the general population, but are present in persons with psychotic disorders. These symptoms are usually acute,

What Nurses Know...

Your affect *is the way you express your emotions, usually by your facial expressions, tone of voice, mannerisms, and posture. For example, if you feel anxious, your affect may be apparent by biting your lip, a cracking voice, and tapping your feet. Your mood and affect should be the same (known as congruence), but there are times for all of us when they don't match. Have you ever been so happy that you cried, or so scared that you laughed? These are examples of your affect being incongruent (not matching) with your mood, and both are perfectly normal.*

often vary over time in severity, and may be absent for long periods. Positive symptoms include hallucinations and delusions. Hallucinations are faulty sensory perceptions, including seeing things that are not really there or hearing voices that no one else can hear. Delusions are faulty ideas, such as believing you are Jesus Christ or that the CIA is out to get you.

Negative symptoms are the absence of thoughts, perceptions, or behaviors that are ordinarily present in the general population and are often stable throughout the life of the disorder. A person with negative symptoms may have a dull affect, which means that they are not very emotionally expressive. The person may also have difficulty with daily activities, such as getting dressed.

Dealing with Psychotic Symptoms

People diagnosed with PTSD can display symptoms such as paranoia that may be viewed as psychotic thinking. However, it is unclear whether these symptoms are a result of the PTSD or of a separate psychotic problem. People diagnosed with a certain disorders, such as bipolar disorder and schizophrenia, can demonstrate symptoms of PTSD. The overlapping in symptoms can be confusing and make accurate diagnosis difficult. Yet accurate diagnosis is important because the treatment for PTSD symptoms radically differs from the treatment for psychotic symptoms. If you have psychotic symptoms, you cannot manage them on your own. Make sure that your therapist and/or healthcare provider conducts a detailed assessment to make sure that you get the proper diagnosis.

Avoidance and Numbing Symptoms

Avoidance and numbing symptoms are clumped together into a criterion for the diagnosis of PTSD. However, they are actually two distinct manifestations.

What Nurses Know...

Avoidance *and* numbing *symptoms include avoiding thoughts, feelings, or conversations associated with the trauma; avoiding activities, places, or people that arouse recollections of the trauma; a sharp decrease in interest or participation in normal activities; feeling numb or not caring about anything; feeling detached from others; restricted range of moods; and a sense of a shortened future.*

AVOIDANCE

Because of the impact of the traumatic event that led to your PTSD, you may do all you can to avoid things that trigger memories of the event. Avoidance is a normal reaction to trauma, but when avoidance becomes extreme or the main coping strategy, it can interfere with your emotional healing.

Avoidance can be either behavioral or emotional. Behaviorally, you may avoid going near the place where the trauma occurred or watching television programs about similar events. If you were traumatized in a certain city, you may have even moved to escape reminders of the event. You may avoid sights, sounds, smells, or people that remind you of the traumatic event. Smell alone can release a flood of memories that can affect your emotional state and performance. The olfactory bulb is part of the brain's limbic system, which is associated with memory and feeling. Smell can bring up memories and powerful responses almost instantaneously. Avoidance can also mean dodging activities that were once enjoyable.

Emotional avoidance is the avoidance of thoughts or feelings about the traumatic event. People with PTSD often attempt to avoid emotions about the trauma and emotions in general. Some people try to distract themselves as one way to avoid thinking about the traumatic event. Disaster survivors may try to think about other things whenever thoughts of the disaster enter their mind, or they may disallow themselves to feel sad about the losses incurred during the event.

"Out of sight, out of mind" may work when you are trying to avoid the temptation of eating chocolate, but it has a negative effect when it comes to avoiding emotions—at least in the long run. Emotional avoidance can worsen your symptoms and make it harder for you to move on with your journey.

Dealing with Avoidance

The opposite of avoid is approach. You need to face your fears. Being in anxiety-producing situations is stressful, but it will help you to develop adaptive ways to deal with your avoidant symptoms. One way you can face fear is through systematic desensitization, a type of therapy that can effectively help reduce the anxiety associated with fearful situations. You begin with imagining yourself in the fearful situation and then work up to real-life situations (within reason, of course). You learn coping skills along the way. Because systematic desensitization is a form of therapy, you do need to talk to your therapist to see if it can be incorporated into your treatment.

NUMBING

Ironically, while people with PTSD can have difficulty with intrusive emotions, they can also experience numbing of their emotions. They may find it difficult to express emotions toward other people or to be in touch with their feelings altogether, an emotional deadness. Emotional numbing is unique among PTSD's symptoms. In contrast with re-experiencing, avoidance, and hyperarousal, which result in negative moods and affect, emotional numbing diminishes moods and affect. The person is disinterested in activities, is detached from others,

What Nurses Know...

Anhedonia is the inability to experience pleasure from activities formerly found enjoyable (socializing with friends, sex, exercise, shopping, hobbies, etc.). It is seen in people with PTSD, as well as other problems, including depression.

and displays a restricted range of emotional expressions. It has been suggested that when a person's efforts to reduce trauma-related distress fail, the affective system shuts down, resulting in numbing symptoms.

You may find it difficult to connect with your feelings or to express emotions toward others. You may feel emotionally numb and disconnected, isolating yourself from friends and family, and you may have lost interest in activities that you once enjoyed. Perhaps you forget or are unable to talk about important parts of the trauma. These are all signs of emotional numbing, as is thinking that you will have a shortened life span or will not reach personal goals.

Dealing with Numbing

Emotional numbing shuts you out from your family, friends, community, and even yourself. To get back your positive feelings, try these suggestions:

- Try art or music therapy, since can both bring about feelings of pleasure. If you are not sure where to find these therapies, talk to your therapist or healthcare provider. You can also use the therapy locator feature on the following national organization websites:
  - American Music Therapy Association: www.musictherapy.org
  - American Art Therapy Association: www.arttherapy.org

- Get a pet. Dogs (cats, too) provide unconditional love and may help you learn to reciprocate without fear. They can also help decrease the loneliness that comes from the inability to connect with people.
- Get involved in activities that you enjoyed in the past, especially those that involve your family and friends because they can serve as a cheering squad to help break the ice.
- Talk to your healthcare provider or therapist about medication. Some antidepressants, including Prozac and Zoloft, may help your emotional numbness by helping with underlying depression. Both of these medications are discussed in detail in Chapter 5.

Increased Arousal Symptoms

Vigilance is a normal response after trauma whereby your mind and body stay alert for any potential threats to your well-being. This is a survival instinct. However, when vigilance goes into hyper mode well after the threat is gone, it becomes a symptom that becomes a threat to your well-being. Hypervigilance is watching or checking of one's surroundings above and beyond what would be considered reasonable. Being watchful for enemy gunfire during combat is reasonable; being watchful for enemy gunfire in the safety of one's home is not. Hypervigilance is the characteristic that makes some people always check under their bed at night, sit with their back to the wall at restaurants, and put multiple locks on their homes, even in safe neighborhoods. When these behaviors become cumbersome, they move beyond reasonable: when the checking becomes obsessive and distressful – when you leave a restaurant because you can't get a seat where you can see the door; or when the abundance of locks creates safety barriers in emergent situations.

Do you feel constantly on guard or all keyed up? In this state, your body expects bad things to happen, and little stressors feel like big ones. You're always on the lookout for danger, at home,

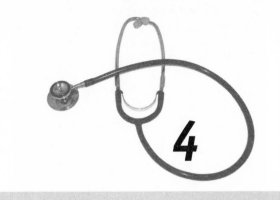

Collateral Damage:
Complications of PTSD

"I sought and paid for my own therapy as an adult in my 30s. My therapist wanted me to confront my mother about her lack of support and denial, but she was becoming a premature 'old lady,' and I chose not to confront her. She died a few syears ago, and I did not attend her funeral, unable to attend because I just had major surgery and could not travel. My siblings never forgave me for staying home on that day. I have pretty much disconnected from all of them. 'Unplugged' is a good word." ABBY

PTSD tends to come with excess baggage that can weigh you down on your life journey. This chapter helps you to identify and understand the different baggage—to see how the various symptoms and their causes overlap and why it is often difficult at best for you to understand what's happening to you.

Many people with PTSD have additional mental health problems, particularly depression, substance abuse, and other anxiety disorders. But you may have related difficulties that are not psychiatric conditions. The symptoms of PTSD, with or without the presence of a co-occurring mental health disorder, can cause havoc in the person's relationships, job, and other life aspects. Finally, because PTSD resulted from trauma, you may also suffer from other aspects of victimization or the aftermath of disaster.

PTSD and Comorbidity

Comorbidity is the presence of two or more disorders simultaneously, a common occurrence in PTSD. For example, if you develop depression because of your PTSD, the depression becomes a comorbid disorder.

DEPRESSION

About 1 in 10 adult Americans suffer from some type of depression, and depression is a common development after trauma. Victims of violent victimization may have difficulty coping with being assaulted; war veterans may feel guilty about their combat experiences; and disaster survivors may have overwhelming grief over their losses. Thus, PTSD and depression often occur together. One study showed that depression was found in almost half of people with PTSD. There are three main reasons for this.

- First, the person may have a genetic tendency, which is similar for both disorders.
- Second, people with depression are more likely to experience trauma than those who do not have depression. People with psychological disabilities are at higher risk for violent victimization because they are seen as easy targets to predators.

● Third, the symptoms of PTSD are so distressing that they can cause depression, and some of them overlap with the symptoms of depression.

Like PTSD, depression can interrupt your life journey on a daily basis and make it hard for you to perform everyday tasks. Depression is more than just feeling a little blue or sad; it is a long-lasting problem that can affect the way you feel and think, and it can affect your eating and sleeping, and you may no longer be able to enjoy things that gave you pleasure in the past. Thus, depression sucks the joy right out of you.

You may have depression if you experience some of the following:

● Sadness, unhappiness, hopelessness, helplessness, worthlessness, guilt, and/or pessimism
● Irritability, anxiety, frustration, and/or restlessness
● Loss of interest or pleasure in normal activities
● Crying spells for no apparent reason
● Thoughts of suicide, suicide attempts
● Difficulty concentrating, remembering details, and making decisions
● Slowed thinking, speaking, or body movements
● Fatigue and decreased energy

What Nurses Know ...

Greif and bereavement may be indistinguishable from depression. If your PTSD was initiated by a significant loss, such as the suicide of a child, you may be in a state of bereavement rather than a state of depression. Make sure to discuss this with your healthcare provider or your therapist.

- Insomnia, early-morning wakefulness, or excessive sleeping
- Reduced sex drive
- Appetite changes (too much or too little)
- Persistent aches or pains, headaches, cramps, or digestive problems

Unfortunately, both PTSD and depression are often chronic among women victimized by intimate partner violence (domestic violence) and can persist many years after the abuse has ended. More troubling is that women who develop PTSD and depression subsequent to interpersonal trauma are at heightened risk for future intimate partner violence victimization. This makes it even more imperative for you to get help for your PTSD and depression if you are currently in a partnership that involves violence.

Dealing with Depression

Your therapist will work with you on managing your depression through therapy and, possibly, medications. But you can help alleviate your depression with these suggestions:

- Eat mood-boosting foods that are rich in omega-3 fatty acids, including fatty fish (salmon, sardines, and anchovies), walnuts, flax, soybeans, and tofu. Not a fan of these foods? Try an over-the-counter omega-3 fatty acid supplement.
- Maintain your relationships with family and friends. Isolation and loneliness worsen depression, so maintaining your close relationships and social activities are important. Depression will make you want to stay home, but forcing yourself to get out and socialize will help you feel better.
- Do things you enjoy: Play with the kids, swim, ski, knit, read, and take long hot baths.
- Get out in the sunshine. Lack of sunlight can increase depression, so get outdoors. But make sure you wear adequate sunscreen.

- Exercise. Start small with moves like walking around the block or walking the dog, and work your way up to 30 minutes a day. Physical activity increases mood-enhancing brain chemicals, raises endorphins, reduces stress, and relieves muscle tension. (Make sure to check with your healthcare provider before beginning an exercise plan.)
- Challenge negative thinking. Use part of your journal as a negative thought log and begin substituting those thoughts for positive ones, and stop using all-or-none thinking by avoiding words like always and never.

SUICIDE

Some say that trauma increases a person's risk for suicide, while others say that it is the presence of PTSD, depression, or both after trauma that increases the risk. Regardless of the reason, you should always be on the lookout for any warning signs of suicidal thinking.

There are a few theories as to why the risk is higher in persons who have been traumatized. One is the presence of PTSD with other mental health problems. Some studies have connected suicide risk to distressing trauma memories, anger, and poor control of impulses of PTSD. Suicide risk is also higher for persons with PTSD who have negative stress-coping styles, such as not expressing feelings. In combat veterans, the strongest link to both suicide attempts and thinking about suicide is guilt related to combat because many veterans have disturbing thoughts and extreme guilt about actions taken during war. These thoughts can be overwhelming, making it hard to deal with the intense feelings. Suicidal thinking should always be immediately assessed by a professional.

BORDERLINE PERSONALITY DISORDER

Borderline personality disorder is a complex psychiatric disorder characterized by unstable personal relationships, intense

WARNING SIGNS OF SUICIDE

If you or someone you know is thinking about suicide, immediately call your local suicide hotline or your therapist, or go to the emergency department.

You can also call:

1-800-SUICIDE (1-800-784-2433)
1-800-273-TALK (1-800-273-8255)—Press 1 if you are a veteran
1-800-799-4TTY (1-800-799-4889)—Hotline for the deaf

Suicidal thoughts, intentions, and attempts should always be taken seriously. Warning signs include:

- *Worsening depression*
- *Sudden change in mood from being depressed to being happy or very calm*
- *Stating "I want to kill myself"*
- *Constantly thinking or talking about suicide*
- *Making comments such as, "You'll never have to worry about me anymore" or "The world would be better off without me"*
- *Being preoccupied with art, music, movies, books, and other media about suicide*
- *Consistent risk raking behaviors*
- *Thinking or talking about being hopeless or worthless*
- *Tying up loose ends (making a will, putting affairs in order)*
- *Giving away meaningful objects*
- *Saying good-bye to loved ones*

anger, feelings of emptiness, and fears of abandonment. People with borderline personality disorder have troubled thinking patterns and always seem to be in crisis. They can be rational and calm one moment, and then explode into inappropriate anger in response in the next. Symptoms of borderline personality disorder may include significant fear of real or imagined abandonment; intense and unstable relationships that fluctuate between extreme love and hate; persistently unstable self-image; self-damaging impulsiveness (uncontrolled spending, promiscuous sex, binge eating, excessive gambling, substance abuse, and reckless driving); repeated suicidal behaviors or threats; self-mutilation (carving, burning, cutting, branding, picking and pulling at skin and hair, biting, and excessive tattooing and body piercing); unpredictable mood swings; persistent feelings of emptiness; and inappropriate anger or trouble controlling anger.

The co-occurrence of borderline personality disorder and PTSD is fairly common. Borderline personality disorder can also result from trauma, especially abuse during childhood. The impulsive behaviors of and unstable relationships resulting from borderline personality disorder can place the person at greater risk for experiencing another traumatic event, especially assault and accidents. The big concern is that the co-occurrence of both of these disorders is associated with poorer functioning. Areas of poorer functioning include greater number of lifetime unwanted sexual events; higher frequency of self-injury episodes; more trauma-related triggers; more co-occurring anxiety

What Nurses Know . . .

Self-injuring behaviors, also called cutting, differ from suicide attempts in that the person does not intend to kill him- or herself. This behavior is often related to trauma, chiefly child abuse. People with PTSD may self-harm to decrease feeling numb or feeling outside their bodies, to reduce anger, to hurt oneself instead of hurting others, and as a call for help.

disorders, especially panic, agoraphobia, and obsessive-compulsive disorder; more difficulty with anger suppression; and less expression of positive emotions.

Dealing with Borderline Personality Disorder

One of the most challenging problems in borderline personality disorder is dealing with emotional pain. The pain can be so unbearable that you may want to drown it with alcohol or literally try to cut it out through self-injury. But these and other negative behaviors are both harmful and ineffective. Therefore, you need more positive ways to ease the pain.

- Call a good friend and talk about what happened that caused the pain. If you don't know why you feel bad, talk about how you feel.
- Write, draw, or paint your emotions. Creative acts can be healing. They help people express hidden emotions, can also reduce stress, fear, and anxiety, and can provide a sense of freedom.
- Use relaxation exercises. Deep breathe, stretch. Imagine yourself in a safe, comforting place.
- Wait it out. Strong emotions are like strong thunderstorms, they tend to pass quickly. Get a stop watch or egg timer and give yourself time out. Sit in another room, set your watch or timer for ten minutes, and wait for the emotion to pass.
- Volunteer. Helping someone else with his or her pain can make you forget about yours.
- Get grounded. Grounding is a set of strategies that help you detach from emotional pain by getting you to focus on your "external world" instead of your "internal world." When you experience emotional pain, you need to disconnect from it so that you can gain control over your feelings and feel safe. Grounding serves double duty because it also helps people with PTSD who feel overwhelmed by emotion or who feel

emotionally numb. Focus on the present, and try these methods to see which works best for you:

- Focus on the details of the room you are in and describe each of them in detail (color, shape texture, size, etc.).
- Describe an everyday activity, such as making a meal from scratch.
- Read a book or magazine out loud.
- Pass an ice cube from hand to hand.
- Take a warm bath or shower.
- Jump rope.
- Keep saying, "I can handle this."
- Play soothing music.

ALCOHOL AND DRUG ABUSE

Substance abuse is among the most prevalent disorders diagnosed in the United States. The occurrence rates of substance abuse are difficult to determine due to the secrecy and illegality of the behaviors associated with the use of unlawful substances. But alcohol is considered to be the most prevalent drug of choice, with an estimated more than 15 million Americans dependent on alcohol alone. The prevalence rates of other substances vary widely.

What Nurses Know...

The term substance dependence *usually describes physical dependence, which refers to the symptoms that result in withdrawal symptoms when alcohol or drugs are stopped.* Addiction *refers to the loss of control over the urges to take the alcohol or drug even at the expense of adverse consequences.*

Alcohol and drug abuse have been shown to be increased in persons with PTSD, and this combination has severe consequences for those individuals in terms of the illness course, symptom severity, and effectiveness of treatment. Substance use relapse may further interfere with the individual's ability to cope effectively with the symptoms of PTSD, which would lead to an increase in both PTSD and substance abuse symptoms and behaviors.

People with both PTSD and substance abuse problems appear to abuse substances related to their specific symptom pattern. Some types of substances are used to self-medicate to relieve symptoms of intrusion, avoidance, numbing, and arousal. Many classes of abused substances are correlated with PTSD, including alcohol, opiates, anti-anxiety medications, pain killers, and cocaine.

If you drink to forget about your trauma or symptoms, realize that drinking only makes it harder to concentrate, to be productive, and to enjoy your life. Alcohol makes it harder to cope with

What Nurses Know...

Traumatized women have more risk for drinking problems, and women in general are at greater risk for developing alcohol-related problems than men. Alcohol moves through the digestive tract and is dispersed into the body's water; thus, the more water available, the more diluted the alcohol. Men usually weigh more than women, so women have less water in their bodies than men. Therefore, a woman's brain and other organs are exposed to more concentrated alcohol and the toxic byproducts when the body breaks down and eliminates alcohol.

stress and your trauma memories and can actually increase your PTSD symptoms. You can worsen the numbing of your feelings, your feelings of being on guard, and your detachment to your family and friends. You may self-medicate with alcohol to try to help you sleep, but too much alcohol can get in the way of restful sleep because it changes the quality of sleep and makes it less refreshing. When you suddenly stop drinking, the nightmares often get worse. Drinking continues the cycle of avoidance, and avoiding the bad memories and dreams actually prolongs the PTSD, slowing the process of your treatment.

Behavioral or cognitive behavioral treatments are effective for both PTSD (prolonged exposure and cognitive processing therapy) and substance abuse (cognitive behavioral therapy, motivational enhancement technique, twelve-step facilitation). However, little is known on treating co-occurring PTSD/substance abuse. Early preferences focused on sequencing treatments. More recently, those in favor of combined treatments see PTSD/substance abuse as one issue and plan treatment accordingly.

Dealing with Substance Abuse

Substance abuse is a broad category and requires specialized treatment. Talk to your therapist about combined treatments for PTSD and substance abuse. In addition, here are some resources that may be helpful.

- Seeking Safety: http://www.seekingsafety.org/
  A present-focused therapy to help people attain safety from trauma/PTSD and substance abuse. The treatment is available as a book, providing both client handouts and guidance for clinicians.
- Boston Consortium Model: Trauma-Informed Substance Abuse Treatment for Women
  http://www.northeastern.edu/bouve/research/IUHR

Table 4.1 Signs of Substance Abuse

Alcohol
Signs of alcohol abuse
- Blackouts
- Drinking in dangerous situations, such as driving a car
- Drinking in the morning
- Family and friends worried about your drinking
- Hurt self or others when drinking
- Keep drinking despite health problems
- Legal problems because of drinking
- Problems at home or work because of drinking

Signs of alcohol dependence or addiction
- Can't quit drinking or control how much you drink
- Drink more often than you want
- Give up other activities to drink
- Make excuses for drinking
- Physical signs of alcohol dependence: weight loss, a sore or upset stomach, redness of the nose and cheeks
- Spend a lot of time drinking
- Withdrawal symptoms: anxiety, nausea, sweating, shaking

Opiates
Opioids are narcotic, pain-killing drugs. Natural opioids are opium and morphine; semi-synthetic opioids include heroin, oxycodone (Oxycontin), and hydrocodone; synthetics include buprenorphine, methadone, fentanyl, meperidine, and codeine.

Signs of abuse and dependence
- Confusion
- Constipation
- Depression
- Needle marks (if injecting drugs)
- Reduced sense of pain
- Sedation
- Slowed breathing

Anxiolytics
Anxiolytics are antianxiety medications including the class Benzodiazepines, which include diazepam (Valium), alprazolam (Xanax), lorazepam (Ativan), clonazepam (Klonopin), and chlordiazepoxide (Librium)

(continued)

Table 4.1 Signs of Substance Abuse (*continued*)

Signs of abuse and dependence
- Anorexia
- Anxiety
- Confusion
- Depression
- Dizziness
- Drowsiness
- Headaches
- Insomnia
- Lack of coordination
- Memory impairment
- Slowed breathing and decreased blood pressure
- Slurred speech
- Weakness

Cocaine
Signs of abuse and dependence
- Decreased appetite
- Depression as the drug wears off
- Euphoria
- Increased heart rate, blood pressure, and temperature
- Insomnia
- Irritability
- Nasal congestion and damage to the mucous membrane of the nose in users who snort drugs
- Paranoia
- Rapid speech
- Restlessness
- Weight loss

This program provides a fully integrated set of substance abuse treatment and trauma-informed mental health services to low-income, minority women with co-occurring alcohol/drug addiction, mental disorders, and trauma histories.

OTHER ANXIETY DISORDERS

PTSD is an anxiety disorder that can be accompanied by other anxiety disorders. While anxiety is a normal human emotion that everyone experiences at times of stress, anxiety disorders cause so much distress that they interfere with your ability to lead a normal life.

General Anxiety Disorder (GAD)

General anxiety disorder is defined as excessive anxiety and worry about several events or activities for a period of six months or more. The person finds the worry hard to control and experiences impairment in important areas of his or her life because of it. The person can't stop worrying about his or her health, money, family, home, school, or job to such a point that life is a constant state of fear and dread. This anxiety expresses itself in physical symptoms:

- Difficulty concentrating, irritability, and an increased startle response
- Shortness of breath, excessive sweating, palpitations, and various gastrointestinal symptoms
- Shakiness, restlessness, and headaches

Other symptoms are an unrealistic view of problems, nausea, needing to go to the bathroom frequently, and sleep problems.

Dealing with General Anxiety

General anxiety adds to the strain of the anxiety you feel from your PTSD. To deal with all this anxiety, be AWARE:

- Accept your anxiety. Don't fight it. Resistance only prolongs its unpleasantness.
- Watch your anxiety. Rate it on a 0-to-10 scale so that you notice that it does, indeed, decrease.

- Act with your anxiety. Behave as if you're anxiety free. Slow down if you have to, but keep going. Facing your anxiety will help reduce your fears.
- Repeat the steps. Keep accepting, watching, and acting until your anxiety levels go down and stay down to a point where they are comfortable for you.
- Expect the best. Think positively. Negative thinking can become a self-fulfilling prophesy.

PANIC DISORDER

Experiencing a panic attack during a traumatic event does not necessarily mean that PTSD will develop, but panic disorder and PTSD can still co-occur. Panic disorder creates feelings of terror that strike abruptly and repeatedly, sometimes with no warning. For many people, attacks are just as likely to occur at home as they are in public. The first attack may be associated with the trauma, but may also be completely spontaneous.

A panic attack usually begins with a 10 minute period of rapidly intensifying symptoms, with the main ones being extreme fear and an impending sense of doom. The person cannot name the source of the fear, which creates confusion and difficulty concentrating. Other symptoms include difficulty breathing,

What Nurses Know ...

Heart disease in women is frequently mistaken for a panic attack that comes with shortness of breath, anxiety, palpitations, and indigestion. When in doubt about your symptoms, seek care without delay to make sure you do not have heart disease.

For more information, go to: Women's Heart Foundation: www.womensheart.org

sense of choking or smothering, nausea, stomachache, chest pain, palpitations (pounding heart beat), sweating, hot flashes, chills, shaking, trembling, and numbness or tingling in the fingers and toes. The heart and breathing symptoms can trigger more fear and may be the focus of the person's attention because they believe that they are about to die. The feelings and beliefs are so intense that the person may go to the emergency department thinking they are having a heart attack.

Most cases of *agoraphobia* are believed to be caused by panic disorder. Persons with agoraphobia avoid situations where they will not be able to get help if needed. Some need to be accompanied by a friend or family member in crowded or closed-in spaces, and some refuse to leave the house. Agoraphobia often improves when the panic disorder is treated.

Dealing with Panic Disorder

People are more likely to seek medical attention for panic attacks than other psychological problem. When told "nothing is wrong" or that the problem is psychological, a person may feel embarrassed or frustrated and not seek any further help. If you have heard these words from a healthcare provider after having a panic attack, don't be embarrassed. Your problem is very real, and it's the healthcare provider who should be embarrassed!

What Nurses Know...

Rapid breathing (hyperventilation) may produce low levels of carbon dioxide in the blood. When this happens, breathing into a paper bag sometimes helps in the short term. However, this old-fashioned treatment has been criticized because it can possibly worsen a panic attack or even be hazardous because it can lower oxygen levels. So don't try it at home!

Don't ignore the help you need, so find another healthcare provider. You need a healthcare provider who will first make sure that your symptoms are not caused by heart disease, thyroid disease, low blood sugar, medication side effects, or other physical problems, and who will then diagnose and treat your panic disorder as a real health problem.

When panic strikes, don't wait for it to worsen. Tell yourself that you are having a panic attack and that it will pass. Get to a safe place, if possible, and deep breathe. When it is over, analyze it. Can you identify your trigger? If not, write down what happened in the hours prior to the attack, so that you can discuss them with your therapist.

PHOBIAS

Anxiety is nonspecific; fear is very specific. A phobia is excessive fear of a specific situation or object. People with phobias feel anxiety almost immediately upon confronting the feared item, but the level of anxiety usually varies with both the degree of proximity to the feared item and the degree to which escape from it is limited. The intensity of the reaction, however, does not always connect predictably with the feared item; for example, a person can react differently to the same closed-in space on different occasions.

The individual's fear may be expressed physically by rapid heart rate, increased blood pressure, tremor, feeling faint or actually fainting, nausea, diaphoresis, and feelings of panic. A full-blown panic attack can occur if the individual believes that escape is impossible.

Social phobia (also called social anxiety disorder) creates excessive fear of embarrassment or humiliation in specific social situations, such as public speaking, asking questions in class, and using a public restroom. General social phobia is a chronic and debilitating disorder characterized by phobic avoidance of most social situations. Anxiety and self-consciousness develop from a fear of being closely watched, judged, or criti-cized by others. Thus, the person is fearful of making mistakes and being humiliated in front of others. This fear may worsen with the lack of social skills or experience in social situations, and people often suffer intense worry about a situation before it even happens, sometimes for days or weeks before the event. Social anxiety can build into a panic attack or cause such extreme distress that the person avoids the dreaded situations altogether.

What Nurses Know...

COMMON PHOBIAS

Acrophobia	fear of heights
Agraphobia	fear of sexual abuse
Algophobia	fear of pain
Androphobia	fear of men
Arachnophobia	fear of spiders
Belenophobia	fear of needles, injections
Claustrophobia	fear of having no escape and being closed in
Disposophobia	"compulsive hoarding"; fear of getting rid of or losing things
Genophobia	fear of sexual intercourse
Glossophobia	fear of public speaking
Haptephobia	fear of being touched
Microphobia	fear of germs
Nosemaphobia	fear of illness
Ophidiophobia	fear of snakes
Thanatophobia	fear of death
Xenophobia	fear of strangers

Dealing with Phobias

Given the nature of phobias, you already know your triggers. However, trying to confront a phobia on your own could be over-whelming. Talk to your therapist about systematic desensitiza-tion, a therapy whereby you will be taught relaxation skills and then given the opportunity to practice those skills through grad-ual introduction to your feared object or situation. Systematic desensitization is often used as part of a cognitive-behavioral therapy program, which is the treatment of choice for PTSD.

EATING DISORDERS

The prevalence of PTSD is higher in persons with anorexia ner-vosa and bulimia nervosa. It is thought that eating-disordered behaviors, especially purging behaviors like self-induced vom-iting, serve to facilitate avoidance of traumatic triggers and to numb the hyperarousal and emotional pain associated with traumatic memories and thoughts. Purging may also promote forgetting parts or the entire traumatic event. Eating disorders are serious, complex chronic disorders, which can be life-threat-ening and thus require medical and psychological attention.

Anorexia nervosa has been called the relentless pursuit of thinness. Affected individuals refuse to maintain a body weight at or above a minimally normal weight for their height and age. They weigh less than one-fifth their normal weight for their height, build and age, yet they firmly believe that they're overweight. Anorectics have intense fear of gaining weight or becoming fat, even when underweight, as well as a disturbance in the way in which their body weight or shape is experienced. This body image disturbance can range from mild to severe. They may be preoccupied with their entire body or a specific body area, such as the abdomen, thighs, and buttocks.

People with bulimia nervosa have recurrent binge eating epi-sodes during which they eat a relatively large amount of food in a short period of time and feeling of out of control during the

binge. These episodes are accompanied by repeated compen-
satory actions to prevent weight gain, including self-induced
vomiting, laxative and/or diuretic abuse, ipecac (medication to
induce vomiting) abuse, fasting, and excessive exercise. Like
anorectics, bulimics are constantly concerned with their body
shape and weight. Bulimic individuals develop an intense preoccupation with food that progressively interferes with their
educational, vocational, and/or social activities. Shame follows their binging, and they're usually quite distressed by their
symptoms. Bulimic individuals are also at risk for impulsive
behaviors such as substance abuse, shoplifting, and promiscu-
ity, increasing their chances for chemical dependency and sexually transmitted diseases.

Dealing with Eating Disorders

Eating disorders create a host of physical complications. Women
with anorexia can develop heart, liver, and kidney damage from
malnutrition. They lose their periods because of decreased body
fat and low estrogen, which, along with low calcium intake, can
lead to osteoporosis long before they reach middle age. At the
very least, self-induced vomiting can cause dental decay, but
it can also lead to erosion of the esophagus and a serious body
salt imbalance, particularly potassium depletion, which can
produce fatal heart problems. Some bulimics resort to using
ipecac to induce vomiting. You may be familiar with this drug
because your healthcare provider may have recommended you
keep it on hand in case of accidental poisoning of your toddlers.
Bulimics, however, tend to take massive dosages that can prove
fatal because ipecac is toxic to the heart. Some bulimics resort
to other purgative measures to lose weight, including laxative
or diuretic (water pill) abuse, diet pills, and even enemas. All of
these can lead to various problems, including dehydration and
electrolyte imbalance.

Given the seriousness of these complications, people with eating disorders require treatment from professionals experienced

in working with these disorders. If you have an eating disorder and your healthcare provider and/or therapist are not experienced in treating it, discuss getting a referral to someone who does specialize in these problems.

PTSD and Its Effect on Important Areas of Functioning

PTSD causes significant distress in one's important areas of functioning. Two critical areas are relationships and employment. Stress in general can also affect your physical health; this is covered in Chapter 8.

RELATIONSHIP WITH YOUR PARTNER

Trauma may change your relationships. The overwhelming circumstances of traumatic events can influence your interactions with family, friends, coworkers, and others. Trauma challenges your sense of safety and security in the world. Your confidence in the future may be shaken; the way you understand the meaning of life may be changed; and the way you think and feel about yourself may be different. Relationships can reflect these feelings in several ways. Symptoms of PTSD can cause problems with trust, closeness, communication, and problem solving, which can affect the way you act with others. And the way your loved ones respond to you can affect you as well, creating a cyclical pattern that may sometimes harm relationships.

Trauma may create expectations of danger, betrayal, or potential harm within new or old relationships. Survivors may feel vulnerable and unsure about what is safe, making it difficult to trust others, even those whom they trusted in the past. You may feel frightened about getting close to people for fear of being hurt, or you may feel angry at the loss of control in your life and become aggressive or controlling toward others. You may become angry because you feel easily threatened. You may feel intense shame, feel unlovable or bad in some way, or feel guilty about what happened to you or about something that you should have done in the traumatic situation. You may feel that no one can truly understand what happened to you, or you may worry that it is a burden to discuss these experiences within a close relationship.

Survivors with PTSD may feel numb and distant from others. You may have less interest in social or sexual activities. If you feel irritable, on guard, jumpy, worried, or nervous, you may not be able to relax or be intimate. You may have trauma memories or flashbacks and go to great lengths to avoid them by avoiding activities that affect your loved ones. If you have trouble sleeping or nightmares, both you and your partner may not be able to get enough rest, making sleeping together harder. Drug and alcohol problems, which may be an attempt to cope with PTSD, can destroy intimacy and friendships and may increase the risk of verbal or physical violence.

Your partner, family members, and friends may feel hurt, cut off, or depressed because you have not been able to get over the trauma. They may become angry or distant, or feel pressured, tense, and controlled. Your symptoms can make your loved ones feel as if they are living in a war zone or in constant threat of danger. Living with someone who has PTSD can sometimes lead your partner to experience some of the same feelings of having been through trauma.

Strengthening Your Relationship with Your Partner

Problems can make or break relationships. Don't let PTSD break yours:

- Assess your readiness to commit to strengthening your partnership bond.
- Recognize that rebuilding relationships with family and friend requires dedication, perseverance, hard work, and commitment.

- Discuss the matter with your therapist to determine if relationship therapy would be beneficial.
- Establish a personal support network that will help you cope with PTSD while you rebuild your relationships.
- Share feelings honestly and openly with respect and compassion.
- Strengthen cooperative problem-solving and communication skills.
- Include playfulness, spontaneity, relaxation, and mutual enjoyment in your relationship.
- Assist your partner in learning how to help you, and ask your partner how you can help him or her.
- Negotiate how much of the trauma will be shared in the relationship.
- Express your appreciation for your partner's love and support.

RELATIONSHIP WITH YOUR CHILDREN

Parenting is difficult under the best of circumstances, and parenting with PTSD, and possibly its comorbidities, can be especially challenging. Your functioning is compromised at times, but that does not mean you can't be a good parent—with a little work. You need to know how your illness impacts your children, how they may respond, and what you can do to be a better parent.

Your re-experiencing symptoms can come out of nowhere with accompanying symptoms of fear, guilt, or anger. These symptoms can be quite frightening and confusing to your children. They can't comprehend what is happening, and may worry about you or that you can't take care of them. If your avoidance symptoms disallow you to do things or go places, your children may feel that you don't care about them. If you are on the edge and cranky most of the time, you may come across as mean and unloving.

Without appropriate parenting skills or intervention, your child will develop negative behaviors. Without your emotional support, your child may develop depression, anxiety, school difficulties, and problems with relationships. Your child may become "parentified" and take on the adult role, filling in for you and giving up his or her childhood. Your child may also start to feel and act just like you, showing symptoms of PTSD, as a way to connect with you. This secondary trauma is also called "intergenerational PTSD." This can also develop when parents teach children not to talk about disturbing events, thoughts, or feelings, or when the parent shares too many details about traumatic events.

Strengthening Your Relationship with Your Children

Good parenting while having PTSD is difficult, but not impossible. Your first step is to explain to your children the reasons for your difficulties, without giving them too much detail. Your children need to understand that the symptoms have nothing to do with them, that they are not to blame. How much you say depends on your child's developmental stage, so you may want to get some assistance from your or your child's healthcare provider. Once you have taken this giant leap in your journey, you may want to:

- Consider family therapy, which can help you while also helping your family members to get their needs met while you are recovering.
- Consider individual therapy for each of your children based on their ages, such as play therapy for the young ones and talk therapy for the older ones.
- Seek out PTSD family support groups in your area.
- Watch for red flags. If you notice unusual behaviors in your children, contact their therapist or healthcare provider before the behaviors worsen.

- Create a crisis plan for emergencies. Plan in advance with those who will care for your children should you be unable due to your illness.
- Enroll your children in activities so they can connect with other healthy children and adults.
- Take care of yourself. You cannot be your parenting best when you are not at your best.

WORK

Your job or career is an important part of you. Besides the obvious issue of providing an income, it also helps you feel better about yourself and gives you a chance to grow as a person. However, having PTSD can make working difficult. Your work environment can be stressful. For example, if you are required to attend meetings, you feel on guard and trapped. A work environment with loud, unexpected noises can trigger a strong startle response. You may need to interact with people that you feel disconnected or detached from. Finally, concentration and sleep problems may make it difficult to be productive and attentive at work.

Strengthening Your Working Abilities
To make work more rewarding:

- Know your work-related triggers and develop a plan to manage them.
- Create a mental image of a typical day at work, and write down all the possible triggers. Then match them up with ways to cope—strategies you learned from your therapist, from your experiences, and from this book.
- Create a support list of names of those you can contact in case you need to talk to someone.

What Nurses Know...

Your PTSD may be considered a disability under the Americans with Disabilities Act (ADA). A person is considered to have a disability if that person has a physical or mental impairment that substantially limits one or more major life activities, a record of such an impairment, or is regarded as having such an impairment. For more information about how to determine whether you have a disability covered by the ADA, visit www.eeoc.gov/policy/docs/902cm.html

PTSD and Victimization

Victimization can have significant and long-lasting effects on victims and their families. Besides psychological trauma, victims may suffer physical, social, and/or financial trauma that can leave them devastated if they do not get proper intervention. Numerous studies have examined the long-term consequences of relationship violence during childhood. These studies have suggested that physical and sexual abuse in early life can lead to problems in adulthood, including poor mental and physical health, as well as higher rates of substance abuse. Few studies have examined the long-term consequences of relationship violence in adulthood. However, these studies have suggested that women who experience relationship violence in adulthood have poor health, including depressive symptoms, impairment with daily living activities, and excessive alcohol consumption. One study showed that relationship abuse was associated with increased hospital admissions.

Physical Effects

The physical effects of abuse vary according to the type of abuse perpetrated and may stem from physical or sexual abuse or from

What Nurses Know...

The mission of the Office for Victims of Crime (OVC) is to assist crime victims. Their website (www.ojp.usdoj.gov/ovc/welcome.html) offers several resources for those who have been victimized by crime.

neglect. Some effects may be short-term, such as bruising or a minor fracture, while others are permanent. Victims may suffer from brain damage from head injury or functional disabilities from spinal cord injuries.

Victims of intimate partner violence may experience broken bones, chronic pelvic pain, abdominal and gastrointestinal problems, frequent vaginal and urinary tract infections, and sexually transmitted diseases, including HIV. Many of the physical injuries sustained by women from intimate partner violence seem to cause chronic health problems as women age. Women have identified arthritis, hypertension, and heart disease as being caused by or aggravated by intimate partner violence early in their adult lives. Disorders such as diabetes mellitus or hypertension may be worsened in victims of intimate partner violence because the abuser may not allow them access to medications or adequate medical care.

Abused women may experience chronic pain such as headaches or back pain, or recurring central nervous system symptoms including fainting and seizures. Many report choking and blows to the head resulting in loss of consciousness, both of which can lead to serious medical problems including neurological problems. Gastrointestinal symptoms (loss of appetite, eating disorders) and gastrointestinal disorders (chronic irritable bowel syndrome) are associated with chronic stress, and these may begin during a violent relationship, be related to child sexual abuse, or both. Gynecological problems are the most consistent, persistent, and most frequent physical health problem in battered women. These include sexually transmitted diseases, vaginal bleeding or infection, fibroids, decreased sexual desire, genital irritation, pain on intercourse, chronic pelvic pain, and urinary tract infections. Forced intercourse may explain the higher prevalence of gynecological problems.

Women exposed to spousal violence may experience still-births or spontaneous abortions. Physical assault during pregnancy can result in placental separation; rupture of the uterus, liver, or spleen; preterm labor; fetal fractures; low-birth-weight babies; and poor prenatal care. Abusive partners may also pressure their wives or girlfriends not to gain weight or lose their figure; such abuse causes stress, which has in turn been associated with smoking, low maternal weight gain, and consequently low birth weight infants.

What Nurses Know...

ORDERS OF PROTECTION

If you are a victim of intimate partner violence and you fear for your safety or that of your children (and pets in some states), you should consider obtaining an order of protection. An order of protection is a legally binding court order that restrains an individual who has committed an act of violence against a person from further acts against that person. Protective orders vary state by state and are called by various names (restraining orders, protection from abuse orders [PFAs], etc.). Most are used to protect against family/intimate partner violence; some jurisdictions use them for strangers. If you feel that an order of protection would be helpful, contact your attorney or your local victims' service agency.

Victims may fear for their lives; in some cases, especially those of intimate partner violence, victims may be in danger of being killed. Offenders may not yet have been caught, or may be out on bail or probation or parole.

Financial Effects

Many victims often lose their jobs because of absenteeism due to injury or illness related to the violence. Absences can also occur from court appearances, which themselves can jeopardize a victim's livelihood. Victims of intimate partner violence and stalking may have to move their homes and families to avoid violence. Besides being costly, this too can interfere with continuity of employment. Victims may also have to forego financial security (i.e., alimony or child support) during divorce proceedings to avoid further abuse, and many therefore become impoverished over time. If you incurred medical expenses or other costs because of victimization, you may be eligible for compensation through your state's Victim Compensation Board. Utilize the resources in the back of this book to find out how to contact them.

PTSD and Homicide Survivors

Losing a family member to homicide is one of the most traumatic events that a person can experience, and PTSD is more common

What Nurses Know...

The National Association of Crime Victim Compensation Boards is a network of professionals in state and local government working together to provide financial assistance for victims of violent crime (www.nacvcb.org).

among homicide survivors than in those who have lost a loved one due to accident or suicide. There is no way to prepare for this tragic event, which leaves tremendous pain and upheaval in its wake and crosses all cultures, races, and genders. Homicide grief experts estimate that there are seven to ten close relatives for every homicide victim, and this does not include significant others, friends, neighbors, and co-workers. Those left behind after homicide are called "homicide survivors." No amount of justice, restitution, prayer, or compassion will bring their loved one back.

When a person is murdered, the death is sudden, violent, and completely incomprehensible. Shared plans and dreams are suddenly and irreparably shattered. The loss will be grieved in different ways by all who felt close to the victim, and grief reactions may be manifested long after the incident. Family members may have had a conflicted relationship with the victim, and the death means that these issues or bad feelings will remain unresolved, leaving the survivor with the additional loss of hope that things could have been worked out while the victim lived. The turmoil and shock is shown by an array of emotional reactions to trauma, including shock, anger, grief, and guilt. Homicide survivors often experience financial hardship due to funeral expenses, medical fees, and mental health counseling. They may feel loss of self, helplessness, loss of control, loss of religion, and loss of safety and security because homicide leaves survivors feeling victimized physically, socially, financially, and spiritually. Homicide survivors also have additional stress created by the presence of the police, media, and involvement with the criminal justice system.

Initially homicide survivors may experience shock and disbelief, numbness, changes in appetite or sleeping patterns, difficulty concentrating, confusion, anger, fear, and anxiety. In cases where family members have not viewed the deceased's body (either because it was not permitted or because they could not bring themselves to do so), it is often difficult for them to accept the reality of the death. Thus, some healthcare professionals urge family members to go through this viewing process, as painful as it may be. Homicide survivors sometimes feel like the whole world stopped, and they cannot understand how everyone else is able to go on about their daily routines.

Later reactions usually include feelings of isolation, helplessness, fear and vulnerability, guilt or self-blame, nightmares, and a desire for revenge. Homicide survivors may experience heightened anxiety or phobic reactions. Their anguish may seem intense and sometimes overwhelming. Some describe a physical pain (lump in the throat) that they feel for several years after the murder.

It is not unusual for homicide survivors to have tremendous feelings of rage toward the perpetrator, and some experience anger toward the victim for getting killed. Depression and hopelessness can lead some homicide survivors to feel that they will ever be happy again. Some may experience suicidal ideation, which warrants immediate attention. Survivors may find themselves suddenly crying over their loss years after the event, a reaction that reflects the depth of the pain. Many say that they know they are doing better when they begin to have more good days than bad days.

Dealing with Being a Homicide Survivor

Both individual and group counseling have been shown to be effective in facilitating the grieving process after a homicide. People well trained to support the family of homicide victims are employed in the criminal justice system. In addition to counseling services located within the community, the justice system supports the families through the homicide investigation and prosecution. The justice system provides services that include accompaniment during court proceedings and notification of any legal activities involving the suspect.

What Nurses Know . . .

Resources for Homicide Survivors:
- *Compassionate Friends: www.compassionatefriends.org*
- *Murder Victims' Families for Reconciliation:* **Error! Hyperlink reference not valid.**
- *National Center for Victims of Crime: Homicide Survivors: www.ncvc.org/ncvc/main.aspx?dbName=DocumentViewer&DocumentID=32358#1*
- *Parents of Murdered Children: http://www.pomc.com*

PTSD and the Aftermath of Disaster

Large-scale natural and man-made disasters cause shock, anguish, anxiety, and various symptoms of acute stress. Victims experience a range of trauma effects, including painful re-experiencing of the event; emotional disconnection; difficulties with short-term memory, concentration, and decision-making; insomnia; hyperarousal; and exaggerated startle reactions. These effects can strain relationships and lead to problems in school and work functioning.

While the impact of disasters is disruptive to everyone involved, most people do not develop long-term problems. However, some people are more at risk than others and will develop PTSD. Besides the general risk factors for PTSD, disaster-specific risks include: loss of family, neighborhood, or community; life-threatening danger or physical harm; exposure to horrible deaths, bodily injuries, or bodies; extreme environmental or human violence or destruction; loss of home or valued possessions; loss of communication with or support from important people in one's life; intense emotional demands; extreme fatigue, weather exposure, hunger, or sleep deprivation;

extended exposure to danger, loss, emotional/physical strain; exposure to toxic contaminants (such as gas, fumes, chemicals, radioactivity, or biological agents).

Natural disasters can be devastating in terms of widespread property loss, as well as death and injury. Terrorism is intentional, meant to destroy, kill, and do harm. Intentional violence creates longer-lasting mental health effects than natural disasters and accidents. Reactions to disasters may be categorized into different phases:

- *Impact Phase*: Several stressors may happen during this phase: encounters with death and threats to life; feelings of helplessness and powerlessness; significant loss; dislocation from family, home, and/or community; feeling responsible, as though the person could have done more; inescapable horror; and human malevolence. Most people react to disaster by trying to protect their lives and the lives of others; some people are stunned and disorganized, and may not be able to protect themselves. Disorganized or apathetic behavior may be transient or may extend into the post-disaster period to the point when some people wander helplessly, possibly indicating a level of dissociation.

- *Immediate Post-disaster Phase* (*Recoil and Response*): Emotional reactions depend on the individual's experience and perceptions of the different stressor elements. Reactions may include: numbness, denial or shock, flashbacks and nightmares, grief reactions to loss, anger, despair, sadness, and hopelessness. However, relief and survival may lead to feelings of elation, which may create feelings of guilt and confusion in the face of the destruction the disaster has wrought. Activities of the rescue may delay these reactions; they may be more apparent as the recovery processes get underway.

- *Recovery Phase*: Once the rescue is completed, the long period of adjustment and return to equilibrium begins for individuals and communities. There may be a honeymoon period

What Nurses Know...

Resources for Disasters
CDC Natural Disaster Resources: www.bt.cdc.gov/disasters
FEMA Disaster Help: www.disasterhelp.gov/disaster-resources.shtm
HUD Disaster Recourses: www.hud.gov/info/disasterre-sources_dev.cfm

that derives from the altruistic and therapeutic community response to the disaster, soon followed by a disillusionment period when the disaster falls from the spotlight, organized support is withdrawn, and the realities of loss, bureaucratic constraints, and the changes created by the disaster must be resolved.

First Responders and PTSD

Are you an EMT, nurse, police officer, or other first responder? So many professional and lay groups and organizations play an important role in the aftermath of disasters that creating a list would risk omitting critical groups. Therefore, the term "first responder" is used here. First responders are regularly exposed to traumatic incidents in the course of their duties, increasing their risk for PTSD. Specific situations include: having to continue responding to calls even after an especially disturbing call, without time to recover or regroup; cumulative stress exposure; feeling helpless in the face of overwhelming demands (a prolonged, failed, rescue; having a colleague or peer killed or seriously injured in the line of duty; the suicide of a peer); being at serious physical risk oneself; witnessing horrifying things; experiencing the death of a child in the line of duty; and responding to a call for help from a victim who is known to the responder.

Dealing with Being a First Responder

The National Center for PTSD recommends that first responders do the following:

- *During a disaster:*
  - Develop a "buddy" system with a coworker.
  - Encourage and support your coworkers.
  - Take care of yourself physically—you can't help others if you are not at your best.
  - Take breaks when needed.
  - Stay in touch with family and friends.
  - Defuse when you experience troubling incidents and after each work shift.
- *After a disaster:*
  - Attend or organize a briefing.
  - Talk about your feelings and listen to those of your coworkers.
  - Get adequate sleep and nutrition.
  - Maintain a normal routine, but decompress gradually.
- *Once back home:*
  - Catch up on your sleep and rest.
  - Get back to your normal pace.
  - Realize that friends and family may not want to hear about the frightening events.
  - Don't worry if you experience mood swing; these will diminish with time.
  - Talk to your children about what happened in their lives while you were gone.
  - Express your feelings: talk, write, paint, exercise; do what works for you.

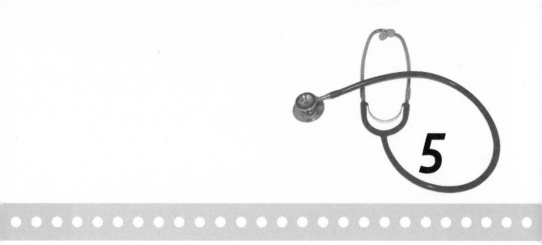

The Usual Suspects: Traditional Treatments for PTSD

"Medications did and still help me to cope as at one point I could not even drive to the local grocery store." CHRIS

You learned about the roadblocks on your journey to wellness, now let's look at the vehicles you can use to drive around those roadblocks—or plow right through them. Vehicles vary. Sometimes you need an 18 wheeler to barrel down the road; other times you do just fine in an economy car. PTSD treatments can vary too. Sometime you just need a little guidance; other times you may need medication.

There are many treatments for PTSD symptoms, but the main approaches are support, encouragement to discuss the event, and education about a variety of coping mechanisms. The emphasis is usually on education about the disorder and its treatment, and the chief treatment methods are psychotherapy, medications, or a combination of both. Because everyone is different, a treatment that works for one person may not work for you. Therefore, it is important for you to be treated by a mental healthcare provider who is experienced in treating PTSD because you may need to try different treatments to find what works best for your symptoms.

Psychotherapy for PTSD

Psychotherapy for PTSD usually lasts 6 to 12 weeks, but can take more time for some people. Several types of psychotherapy can help people with PTSD. Some target the symptoms of PTSD directly, while other therapies focus on social-, family-, or job-related problems. The therapist may combine different therapies depending on your needs.

Psychotherapy teaches you helpful ways to react to the situations or events that trigger your PTSD symptoms. Based on this central goal, different types of therapy may:

● Teach you about trauma and its effects.
● Use relaxation and anger management skills.
● Provide tips for better sleep, diet, and exercise habits.
● Help you identify and deal with guilt, shame, and other feelings about the event.
● Focus on changing how you react to your PTSD symptoms.

What Nurses Know...

If you are worried about what people will think about your getting treatment, consider joining a PTSD support group. You will meet other people with PTSD, which will help you feel less alone, and you can learn tips on how to deal with people who look negatively at therapy.

COGNITIVE BEHAVIORAL THERAPY

Cognitive behavioral therapies are considered first-line treatments for PTSD. Cognitive behavioral therapy methods focus on helping you reprocess the traumatic event. They reduce the degree to which trauma reminders create your strong emotional responses. Treatments typically include a number of components, including education, anxiety management, gradual exposure with desensitization to your triggers, and cognitive restructuring to replace faulty thoughts with healthy ones.

"Cognitive" refers to thoughts and how they can be distorted and lead us to develop inaccurate perceptions of what's going on around us. For example, PTSD may cause you to think that you are re-experiencing the trauma again due to your own distorted impressions of current events. "Behavioral" focuses on actions and how these are tied to thoughts. An example would be avoiding places that remind you of the trauma. Therapists work to enable you to combine the two components to help weaken the connections between faulty thoughts and certain behaviors.

Cognitive behavioral therapy is a goal-oriented, short-term process, which means that you will have about 12 to 20 sessions that predominantly focus upon the present and future. The therapy trains your thought-behavior cycle by reinforcing healthy thinking and appropriate behavioral responses to situations

What Nurses Know...

There are several guidelines that offer recommendations for the treatment of PTSD. These guidelines come from different federal agencies and professional organizations, including the Institute of Medicine. All of the guidelines recommend cognitive behavioral therapy as the most effective treatment for PTSD.

encountered in everyday life. Unlike traditional psychotherapy, cognitive behavioral therapy does not involve lengthy time-frames or extensive digging into your past life events. This is not a "lie on the couch and tell me everything that happened since you were two" type of therapy!

Treatment begins with the therapist asking questions about your symptoms, your relationships, your work, and your family. Chapter 7 provides you with tools that can help you gather information before you make that first appointment. It also will help you choose the right therapist.

You need to develop a trusting bond with your therapist, something that is called the "therapeutic relationship." Establishing a strong, working relationship between you and your therapist is a key feature in cognitive behavioral therapy, because you will work together to develop treatment goals and plans. Your therapist will educate you about the nature of PTSD, and will also explain the cognitive behavioral therapy treatment of choice. This education helps to reduce self-blame and enhance your motivation for change.

Your therapist will teach you how to monitor your thoughts and behaviors. This typically requires that you keep a journal or diary of your symptoms that will include:

• Dates and times the symptoms occur

- The level of discomfort caused by the symptoms (usually on a scale of 1 to 10, with 1 being the mildest amount of discomfort and 10 being the highest)
- The trigger (the event, place, object, or person that set off the symptoms)
- The consequence (what happened because of the symptoms)

Self-monitoring helps you to become aware of the occurrence and timing of target symptoms, as well as the content of your thoughts. Once you identify these thoughts, the therapist will challenge you on their accuracy and what they mean to you.

With cognitive behavioral therapy, you will monitor your symptoms which will also monitor your progress. The journal will allow you to see that your symptoms are becoming less

SAMPLE OF A DAILY JOURNAL ENTRY

Symptom	Date	Time	Level of Distress	Trigger	Consequence
I felt like I could not breathe. My heart was pounding and my stomach was in knots. I knew I just could not go to moves with my friends.	February 21	8 PM	Severe, panicky. I rate it a 9 out of 10!	The movie was a police thriller, and I was afraid that there may be something in it that would remind me of the assault.	This was the third time in a row I canceled with my friends. I worry that they may get sick of me and stop wanting to be with me altogether.

What Nurses Know...

To find a cognitive behavioral therapist, talk to your health-care provider or use the therapist locator feature on the National Association of Cognitive Behavioral Therapists website: http://nacbt.org/searchfortherapists.asp

frequent and less severe. Seeing progress "in print" helps to make it more real, which, in turn, motivates you to keep getting better.

As mentioned earlier in this chapter, there are several types of cognitive behavioral therapy. Your therapist may use one or more of these to help you recover. Here are some that are commonly used for PTSD.

- *Exposure therapy* helps you face and control your fear by exposing you to the trauma you experienced, but in a safe way to avoid re-traumatizing you. For some people with PTSD, trauma memories or reminders can be challenged all at once in a process called *flooding.* For other persons, it is preferable gradually work toward the severe trauma. This is done by using relaxation techniques, and either starting with less upsetting life stressors or by taking the trauma one piece at a time through a process called *desensitization.* Exposure therapy also requires creating mental images of the trauma, writing about it, or visiting the place where the traumatic event happened. Your therapist uses these tools to help you cope with your feelings.
- *Cognitive restructuring* helps you make sense of the bad memories. Sometimes people remember the event differently than how it happened. Negative thoughts and self-talk can block us from taking steps to achieve our goals. Positive

thoughts and self-talk can activate our energies and help us take steps toward our goals. If you feel guilt or shame about things that are not your fault, your therapist may use cognitive restructuring to help you view what happened in a more realistic way.

• *Stress inoculation training* aims to reduce PTSD symptoms by teaching you how to reduce anxiety. Like cognitive restructuring, this treatment helps you look at your memories in a healthy way. Stress inoculation training was first developed as an anxiety management treatment and was later modified for use with sexual assault survivors. It includes education

STRESS MANAGEMENT TRAINING TECHNIQUES

1. Breathing Retraining: *You learn, practice, and master exercises for deep breathing from your diaphragm.*
2. Relaxation Training: *You learn and master the skill of relaxing all your major muscle groups by creating and releasing muscle tension.*
3. Role Playing: *You and your therapist act out successful strategies that help you cope with anxiety provoking situations.*
4. Thinking about and Changing Behaviors: *You imagine successfully coping in stressful situations.*
5. Learning to Talk to Yourself: *You focus on you by talking to yourself. This helps you to recognize negative or unhelpful statements about yourself and to replace them with more helpful "talking."*
6. Stopping Negative Thoughts: *Under the safe supervision of your therapist, you think about the feared situation and then interrupt those thoughts with a distraction. In the beginning, the distraction is the therapist loudly clapping or saying "stop." Later, you will be the one to mentally say stop.*

as well as anxiety management techniques, and it is based on the idea that trauma-related anxiety affects your day-to-day life. By using anxiety management techniques, you can learn to cope more effectively with anxiety. The specific stress inoculation training techniques vary, but usually include: breathing retraining; muscle relaxation training; role playing; thinking about and changing negative behaviors; learning to talk to yourself; stopping negative thoughts; and assertiveness training.

EMDR (EYE MOVEMENT DESENSITIZATION AND REPROCESSING)

EMDR is a newer psychotherapy method that can be very effective in treating PTSD. This therapy was developed by psychologist Dr. Francine Shapiro after she accidentally noticed that eye movements can reduce the intensity of disturbing thoughts. This happened when she realized that her own stress decreased when her eyes moved back and forth as she walked through a park one day.

Essentially, EMDR involves your recalling the trauma and reprogramming that memory in a positive manner while using rapid eye movements to help the process. During a typical EMDR therapy session, you concentrate on your traumatic memory and its negative emotions and beliefs. As you concentrate, your therapist moves his or her finger back and forth, like a windshield

What Nurses Know...

EMDR focuses on intensely stressful subjects. If you are pregnant, or if you have eye problems, a heart condition, or another health problem, consult your healthcare provider before beginning EMDR.

wiper, while your eyes move back and forth following his or her finger. This therapy appears to "unfreeze" your traumatic memory, allowing you to resolve it.

EMDR works quickly; however, you do need to work through its eight phases:

- *Phase 1 (History and Planning Phase)* is when your therapist first determines if you are ready for EMDR and then develops a treatment plan. The therapist will begin by asking about the problems that brought you to therapy, but, unlike other therapies, you will not be asked to talk about your trauma in great detail. Next, you and your therapist will identify possible targets for EMDR processing. Targets may include recent distressing events, current situations that cause emotional distress, related past incidents, and the development of specific skills and behaviors that will be needed by you in future situations. This phase is generally completed in one or two sessions.
- *Phase 2 (Preparation Phase)* is when the therapist ensures that you have good coping skills and that you are in a relatively stable state. If you need further stabilization or additional skills, the therapy focuses on providing them. You should then be able to use stress-reducing techniques whenever necessary, both during and between sessions. The preparation phase usually takes one to four sessions, but sometimes takes longer for people who have suffered significant trauma.
- *Phase 3 (Assessment)* uses three steps to help you work on your targets.
  - *Step 1*: You select a specific picture or scene that best represents the trauma target.
  - *Step 2*: You identify a negative self-belief associated with the trauma, such as "I am still in danger."
  - *Step 3*: You pick a positive statement that you would rather believe, such as "I am safe now."

Once these steps have been successfully completed, your therapist will have you rate your positive feeling. He will use the Validity of Cognition (VOC) scale, which has a scale from 1 to 7. A rating of 1 equals "completely false," and 7 equals "completely true." You will also be asked to identify the negative emotions and physical sensations that you associated with the target.

Examples: I'm a good person   (false) 1 - 2 - 3 - 4 - 5 - 6 - 7 (true)
I'll never get over it   (false) 1 - 2 - 3 - 4 - 5 - 6 - 7 (true)

Your therapist will also use the Subjective Units of Disturbance (SUD) scale, and you will rate your feelings from 0 (no anxiety, feeling peaceful) to 10 (the worst feeling you've ever had; feeling overwhelmed).

- *Phase 4 (Desensitization)* focuses on your disturbing emotions and sensations, using your SUDs ratings. During desensitization, you focus on an image and its resulting negative beliefs, emotions, and body sensations. While you have these in your mind, the therapist leads you through sets of eye movements. You again follow your therapist's fingers with your eyes from side to side, for 15 or more seconds. You then take a deep breath and talk about what you thought and felt during the process. This process is repeated many times until your SUD-scale levels are reduced to 0 or 1.
- *Phase 5 (Installation)* increases the strength of your positive beliefs. You will pair a positive self-statement (such as "I'm a good person") with your original traumatic image, using eye movements. The goal is for you to accept the full truth of your positive beliefs to a level of 6 to 7 on the VOC.
- *Phase 6 (Body Scan)* begins after your positive belief has been strengthened and "installed" in your mind. Your therapist will ask you to think about the trauma target to see if you experience any body tension. If you do, these physical sensations are targeted with more eye movements until the tension disappears. An EMDR session in Phase 6 is not considered

successful until you can think about the original target without feeling any body tension.

- *Phase 7 (Closure)* makes sure that you end each session feeling better than you did at the beginning. If the processing of the traumatic target event is not complete in a single session, your therapist will help you use a variety of self-calming techniques so that you regain a sense of balance. You are in control throughout the EMDR session, and it is important that you continue to feel in control outside the therapist's office. You are told what to expect between sessions, how to use a journal to record these experiences, and which techniques you might use on your own to feel calmer.

- *Phase 8 (Re-evaluation)* takes place at the beginning of every new EMDR session. Your therapist will make sure that the positive results (low SUD levels, high VOC levels, and no body tension) have been maintained. Your therapist will also identify any new areas that need treatment, and will continue to reprocess the additional targets. The Reevaluation Phase is vital to determine the success of your treatment over time.

You may feel relief almost immediately with EMDR, but it is very important to complete the eight phases of treatment.

PSYCHODYNAMIC THERAPY

Psychodynamic psychotherapy helps you examine your personal values and how trauma-related behavior and experience

What Nurses Know...

For more information on EMDR:
EMDR Institute, Inc.: www.emdr.com
EMDR Network: www.emdrnetwork.org

affect them. Psychodynamic therapy focuses on the "unconscious mind" and on things that may influence or cause PTSD symptoms, such as early childhood experiences, current relationships, and what you do to protect yourself from upsetting trauma-related thoughts and feelings.

Brief psychodynamic psychotherapy focuses on the emotional conflicts caused by the traumatic event. You retell the traumatic event to your therapist and achieve a greater sense of self-esteem. You also develop effective ways of thinking and coping, and you more successfully deal with the intense emotions that emerge during therapy. Your therapist also helps you identify current life situations that set off traumatic memories and worsen PTSD symptoms. Brief psychodynamic psychotherapy can help you:

- Build your self-esteem
- Identify your triggers, including stressful memories and other symptoms
- Be more aware of your thoughts and feelings, so you can change how you react to them
- Find ways to deal with intense feelings about the past

FAMILY THERAPY

PTSD can affect your entire family. Your partner and children may not understand why you are under so much stress or why

What Nurses Know...

Researchers have not studied PTSD psychodynamic therapy as much as they have PTSD cognitive behavioral therapy. However, they have found positive effects from psychodynamic therapy, including increased confidence, improvement in relationships, and a decrease in PTSD symptoms.

you sometimes get irritated. They may feel frightened, guilty, or even angry about your disorder. If PTSD is causing trouble within your family, you may wish to discuss with your therapist the possibility of family therapy in addition to your individual therapy.

The purpose of family therapy for persons with PTSD is to help your family communicate, maintain good relationships, and cope with tough emotions. Your family can also learn more about PTSD and how it is treated. During family therapy, each family member can express his or her fears and concerns. You can and should be honest about your feelings and listen carefully to the feelings of others. You can talk about your PTSD symptoms and what triggers them, and you can discuss critical factors of your treatment and recovery. In this way your family will be better prepared to help you.

GROUP PSYCHOTHERAPY

Group therapy has been beneficial for PTSD victims, especially combat veterans and victims of abuse and assault. Being in a group with others who have experiences similar to yours allows you to see that you are not alone. You can get a sense of validation knowing that there are others who have similar difficulties coping with their PTSD symptoms. Trauma survivors can share traumatic experiences and memories more comfortably within the safety, cohesion, and empathy provided by other survivors. It is also usually easier to accept confrontation from a fellow trauma sufferer than from a professional therapist who never went through such experiences firsthand.

Group therapy allows you to learn from others. You can find out from others which coping strategies worked for them and which did not. You can also see that people recover from their PTSD, which can give you hope to recover from yours. But group therapy goes both ways, so you will also be able to help others by

What Nurses Know...

Telling your story (called the "trauma narrative") during group therapy helps you to face the anxiety, grief, and guilt related to that trauma. This helps you to go on with your life instead of getting stuck in the past.

sharing your experiences, which, in the long run, can boost your self-esteem.

Group therapy can also be stressful if you at not at a point where you are comfortable sharing your feelings with others. You should discuss this treatment option with your therapist or healthcare provider before joining a support group.

Medications

Medications can be helpful in treating PTSD symptoms, as well as the possible co-occurring disorders, such as depression. The following symptoms may benefit from medication therapy:

- Re-experiencing symptoms, including nightmares, unwanted thoughts of the traumatic events, and flashbacks
- Avoidance symptoms, including avoiding triggers for traumatic memories such as places, conversations, or other reminders. The avoidance may generalize to other previously enjoyable activities
- Hyperarousal symptoms, including sleep problems, concentration problems, irritability, increased startle response, and hypervigilance

Medications are not a quick fix or cure all, but they can be effective in decreasing the distressing and debilitating symptoms.

However, there are often barriers that keep people from taking medications or taking them properly. These include:

- Fear of possible side effects
- Feeling that medication is a "crutch" and that taking it is a sign of weakness
- Fear of becoming addicted
- Inadherence, such as taking the medication only when symptoms get severe
- Not being sure how to take the medication
- Keeping several pill bottles around and not remembering when the last dosage was taken
- Self-medicating or mixing alcohol or other drugs with prescribed medications

If you have concerns about any of these issues, talk to your healthcare provider.

GENERAL MEDICATION SAFETY TIPS

- *Learn all about your medications: name, dosage, why you are taking it, potential side effects, and any medication-specific information, such as the need to take it on an empty stomach or with meals.*
- *Keep taking your medications, even if you feel better. Your symptoms may come back if you stop.*
- *Carry identification, like a card or ID bracelet, that lists all your medications.*
- *Keep your medications where you will notice them but where they are out of reach of children and pets.*
- *Set a routine to take your medication by attaching it to a common activity, such as eating, brushing your teeth, or going to bed, depending on the medication instructions.*

> • *Use a pill reminder container, even if you only take one pill a day. Doing so allows you to see at a glance whether or not you took your medication. There are many versions of pill containers, including ones for on the go, and most can be found at your local pharmacy.*
> • *Use an alarm, such as the one on your Smartphone, to remind you to take your pills.*
>
> *You may also want to keep a journal of your medication to help you see whether or not it is helping your symptoms.*

Several classifications of medications can help improve symptoms of PTSD. These are antidepressants, anti-anxiety medications, and antipsychotics. The medication Minipress (generic name prazosin) may also be helpful.

ANTIDEPRESSANTS

Antidepressants can help both anxiety and depression symptoms, as well as sleep problems and concentration difficulties. They are especially helpful if you have co-occurring depression or a history of substance abuse.

Selective Serotonin Reuptake Inhibitors (SSRIs)

Selective serotonin reuptake inhibitors (SSRIs) are the most commonly prescribed medications for PTSD and the

What Nurses Know...

Antidepressant medicines may increase suicidal thoughts or actions in some children, teenagers, and young adults when the medicine is first started.

group of medications approved for PTSD by the Federal Drug Administration (FDA). These medications can decrease the anxiety, depression, and panic associated with PTSD and may also help reduce impulsivity, aggression, and suicidal thoughts that can occur in PTSD.

SSRIs decrease depression by blocking the reabsorption of the brain chemical serotonin. Changing the balance of serotonin seems to help brain cells send and receive chemical messages that boost mood. SSRIs are called selective because they seem to affect serotonin and no other brain chemicals.

SSRIs usually take about 6 to 8 weeks to work, so be patient and give them a chance to "kick in." You may also not respond adequately to the first prescribed SSRI and may need to try another. Work closely with your prescriber (whether that is your therapist or primary care provider) to ensure you are getting the medication that works best for you. There are several different SSRIs; here are some of the more commonly prescribed ones, with their generic names in parentheses: Zoloft (sertraline); Celexa (citalopram); Paxil (paroxetine), and Prozac (fluoxetine).

SSRIs can interact with other medications, so make sure to keep your primary healthcare provider and therapist up to date on all your other medications, including over-the-counter medications and herbal medicines.

TIPS FOR TAKING SSRIs

- *Tell your prescriber if you are pregnant or wish to become pregnant, or if you are breast feeding. Some antidepressants can harm your unborn baby if you take them during pregnancy or while you're breast-feeding. For example, Paxil may increase the risk of birth defects, including heart and lung problems.*
- *Tell your healthcare provider and therapist about any other medications or supplements that you are taking. Some*

antidepressants can cause dangerous and even fatal reactions when combined with certain medications or herbal remedies.

- *Take your medication at the same prescribed time(s) every day.*
- *Do not exceed the recommended dosage.*
- *You may experience drowsiness, dizziness, nervousness, agitation or restlessness, insomnia, weight gain, nausea, dry mouth, headache, diarrhea, increased sweating, and rash. Males may also experience erectile dysfunction (inability to maintain an erection).*
- *Report any severe nausea, vomiting, increased depression, or thoughts of suicide to your healthcare provider.*
- *SSRIs can infrequently cause dangerously high levels of serotonin, resulting in serotonin syndrome. This most often occurs when two medications that raise serotonin are combined, such as other antidepressants, medications for certain health conditions, and the herbal supplement St. John's wort. Symptoms of serotonin syndrome include confusion, rapid or irregular heart rate, dilated pupils, fever, and unconsciousness. If you have any of these symptoms, seek medical attention immediately.*

ATYPICAL ANTIDEPRESSANTS

Atypical antidepressants don't fit into other classes of antidepressants. They are each unique medications that each work in different ways. Like other types of antidepressants, atypical antidepressants affect brains chemicals, including dopamine, serotonin, and norepinephrine. Changing the balance of these chemicals seems to help brain cells send and receive messages and boost the person's mood. Atypical antidepressants used for PTSD include: Remeron (mirtazapine), Effexor (venlafaxine), and Serzone (nefazodone). These are also effective in treating co-occurring depression.

TIPS FOR TAKING REMERON

- *Take as prescribed and do not abruptly stop taking this medication without consulting your healthcare provider.*
- *Avoid using alcohol or sleep-inducing drugs while on this medication.*
- *Avoid prolonged exposure to sunlight or sunlamps, and use sunscreen if exposure is unavoidable.*
- *You may experience side effects that include: constipation, dizziness or lightheadedness, dry mouth, increased appetite, increased cholesterol, increased or decreased blood pressure, low white blood cell count, sleepiness, weakness, and weight gain.*
- *Report fever, flulike symptoms, any infections, dry mouth, difficulty urinating, excessive sedation, and suicidal thoughts to your healthcare provider.*

TIPS FOR TAKING EFFEXOR

- *Take with food to decrease stomach upset. Do not crush, cut, or chew capsules; swallow them whole.*
- *Avoid using alcohol or sleep-inducing drugs while on this medication.*
- *You may experience side effects that include: dizziness, drowsiness, loss of appetite, nausea, vomiting, dry mouth, constipation, and tremor.*
- *Report rash, hives, increased depression, and suicidal thoughts to your healthcare provider.*

TIPS FOR TAKING SERZONE

- *Know that the manufacturer warns against drinking alcohol while taking Serzone.*
- *Take as prescribed and do not abruptly stop taking this medication without consulting your healthcare provider.*
- *You may experience side effects that include: dry mouth, sleepiness/sedation, nausea, dizziness, visual problems, weakness, lightheadedness, confusion, orthostatic hypotension (blood pressure drops when getting up from lying down or sitting).*

ANTIPSYCHOTICS

Antipsychotic medications include Zyprexa (olanzapine) and Risperdal (risperidone). Antipsychotics were originally developed for patients with psychotic disorders, such as schizophrenia. However, they are now used for many other psychiatric disorders, including PTSD. Antipsychotic medications work primarily on specific brain chemicals and are used in PTSD to improve hyperarousal and re-experiencing of symptoms. Your healthcare provider or therapist may prescribe a short course of antipsychotics to relieve severe anxiety and related problems, such as difficulty sleeping or emotional outbursts.

The newer antipsychotic medications are generally preferred because they pose a lower risk of debilitating side effects than do "old-fashioned" ones. However, even though the risk is less, there is still a small risk of developing side effects. Antipsychotic medications can have powerful side effects, some of which can be life threatening. For example, a condition called neuroleptic malignant syndrome is a serious complication of antipsychotic medications. Despite its name, this is not a cancer – it is a rare but potentially fatal reaction to antipsychotic medications. Symptoms are high fever, muscle stiffness, paranoid thinking, major changes in blood pressure, excessive sweating, and excessive salivation. However, most common side effects can be managed and usually disappear after a few days. The common side effects include:

- Blurred vision
- Drowsiness
- Dizziness when changing positions
- Sensitivity to the sun
- Skin rashes
- Rapid heartbeat
- Menstrual problems

SERIOUS SIDE EFFECTS OF ANTIPSYCHOTIC MEDICATIONS

Extrapyramidal side effects *(EPS) include tremors, slurred speech, muscle weakness, anxiety, distress, and paranoia.*

Tardive dyskinesia *(TD) involves involuntary movements of the tongue, lips, face, trunk, arms, and legs.*

Neuroleptic malignant syndrome *(NMS) refers to the combination of very high body temperature, paranoid thinking, major changes in blood pressure, excessive sweating, and excessive salivation.*

If you experience any of these symptoms while taking an antipsychotic medication, contact your prescriber immediately.

TIPS FOR TAKING ANTIPSYCHOTIC MEDICATIONS

- *Use caution when driving and using heavy machinery. The medication may make you drowsy.*
- *Don't drink alcohol. Alcohol can increase the effect of your medication, and your medication can increase the effect of alcohol.*

- *Talk to your prescriber if you are pregnant or planning to become pregnant. Safe use of these drugs during pregnancy has not been established.*
- *Don't abruptly stop taking the medication if you have been on it for a long time (4 weeks or more). This may cause withdrawal symptoms, such as headache, stomachache, and dizziness.*
- *Use sunblock and wear protective clothing when outdoors. Your skin is more likely to get sunburned when you take antipsychotic medications.*
- *Get up slowly when lying down or sitting to prevent a sudden drop in your blood pressure and resulting dizziness.*
- *If your mouth gets dry, try sipping water, chewing sugarless gum, or sucking on sugarless hard candy.*
- *Quit smoking. Smoking can affect your medication dosage.*
- *Dress properly in hot or cold weather because your body temperature may be harder to maintain when you take this medication.*

ANTIANXIETY MEDICATIONS

Antianxiety medications can improve feelings of anxiety and stress. They are usually used only for relieving acute anxiety on a short-term basis because they can be habit-forming. These medications are not a good choice if you've had problems with alcohol or drug abuse. Antianxiety medications include Ativan (lorazepam), Klonopin (clonazepam), and Xanax (alprazolam). These medications can cause side effects that include drowsiness, reduced coordination, and problems with balance and memory.

TIPS FOR TAKING ANTIANXIETY MEDICATIONS

- *Don't drive or operate heavy machinery. Drowsiness may occur.*
- *Don't abruptly stop taking the medication. If you do, you may have withdrawal symptoms, such as depression, anxiety, insomnia, muscle cramps, and sweating.*
- *Don't use alcohol while taking an antianxiety medication, because the combination can increase side effects like drowsiness.*
- *Rise slowly from a lying or sleeping position to prevent a sudden drop in your blood pressure and the dizziness that goes with it.*
- *Contact your healthcare provider immediately if you experience sore throat, fever, easy bruising, unusual bleeding, and restlessness. Antianxiety medication may cause blood problems.*

MINIPRESS

Minipress (prazosin) may help insomnia or recurrent nightmares. Minipress, which has been used for years to treat hypertension, blocks the brain's response to norepinephrine. Side effects include dizziness, weakness, stomach upset, dry mouth, and stuffy nose. Men may also experience impotence. The side effects tend to be temporary.

TIPS FOR TAKING MINIPRESS

- *Take the medication as directed. You may need to take the first dose before bedtime.*
- *Use caution when driving or using heavy machinery, as weakness may occur.*
- *Be alert for possible weakness, which may be felt in the early morning, when changing position, and in hot weather. Also use caution when climbing stairs.*

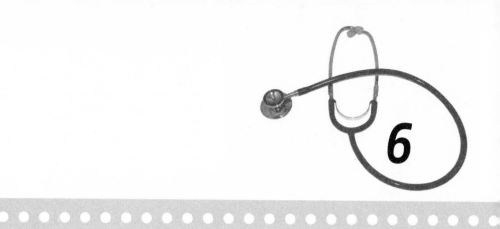

Different Strokes: Alternative Treatments for PTSD

"To cope, I sketched, despite having no artistic ability. I drew the scenes that bothered me. The first sketch series I named Transplanting a Daughter. The second I started 6 weeks before she died but decided to sketch those tiny short happy times. I called this one The Death of a Daughter. Then the grief hit, one year and over 200 sketches later I finished The Grief of a Mother. The last 25 or so [sketches] expressing the most horrific events and the anger I felt at others. These sketches helped me to express my feelings and I don't need to constantly feel those emotions any longer." CHRIS

Sometimes traditional medicine is not enough. Sometimes you just want to try something different. There are many roads to wellness, so you may want to consider an alternate route.

What Nurses Know...

Integrative medicine *is a new term for combining conventional and alternative treatments. It is a holistic form of treatment that encompasses the mind, body and soul.*

Complementary and Alternative Medicine, commonly known as CAM, is a vast group of nontraditional treatments that range from nutritional supplements to biofeedback to pet therapy. Even chiropractic and massage therapy are considered CAM, despite their popularity.

"Alternative" means that the treatments are not typically used in Western medicine. Western medicine refers to the traditional healthcare system in countries like the United States, Canada, the United Kingdom, and Australia. "Complementary" means that a particular alternative treatment is used in addition to traditional Western medicine. There are approximately 1,800 alternative therapies practiced all over the world, and many of them have been around for more than thousands of years.

CAM practices may, over time, become widely accepted by the healthcare community. They are certainly well accepted by the public. The National Center for Complementary and Alternative Medicine reports that 36% of U.S. adults age 18 years and over use some form of CAM.

PTSD and Complementary and Alternative Medicine

CAM approaches to treatment have been utilized for many medical and mental health diagnoses, including PTSD, even though

What Nurses Know ...

People chose CAM for a variety of reasons:
• *Belief that Western medicine is inadequate for their needs*
• *Concern about the safety of medications*
• *Seeing CAM as less invasive than Western medicine*
• *Lack of trust in doctors or bad experiences with the medical world*
• *Religious beliefs*
• *Desire for engaging more holistic treatment*
• *Curiosity*

the research base to support their effectiveness is not yet fully developed. Acupuncture (a component of traditional Chinese medicine), Yoga Nidra (a relaxation and meditative form of yoga), and herbal or dietary supplements have been used for the treatment of PTSD and have been studied, but there is insufficient evidence to draw firm conclusions about their effectiveness for PTSD.

If you are considering using CAM to help your PTSD symptoms, please realize that "natural" does not mean "harmless." Some CAM treatments can interact with medications; for example, St. John's wort can reduce the effectiveness of birth control pills and cause severe agitation if taken with antidepressants. Regardless of the type of CAM you choose, consider these suggestions before you use it:

● Do your homework and research your method of choice. The Internet is full of helpful information, but it is also full of junk. Be cautious of the sites you use. Make sure that they come from reliable professional organizations and institutions, such as the American Academy of Family Physicians, the Mayo Clinic, and, of course, the National Center for Complementary and Alternative Medicine.

- Talk to your healthcare provider before you try anything, especially if you are currently on psychiatric medication and are considering taking herbal medicine. The combination of the two may have a harmful effect. Your healthcare provider may be able to answer your questions and refer you to a CAM practitioner. Your provider may also have enough education and experience with CAM to prescribe it for you.
- If your healthcare provider cannot help you, try these alternatives:
  - Ask a friend who has successfully used the CAM you are considering, but use this as a starting point and find out where your friend obtained reliable information.
  - Check with a nearby hospital or regional medical center.
  - Talk to the director of the nearest nursing or medical school.
  - Check with your state licensing board. Some CAM professions require licensure. These include chiropractic, massage therapy, and acupuncture.
  - Contact the professional organization of your CAM of choice.
- Once you find a CAM practitioner, make sure that the practitioner is the right one for you by doing some research such as the practitioner's:
  - Education
  - Experience

What Nurses Know . . .

While certain types of CAM may be helpful for your PTSD symptoms, realize that the science is not there—yet. The effectiveness of these therapies has not yet been supported by research. If you use CAM, keep your healthcare provider informed—before, during, and after.

- Certification and/or licensure
- Cost
- Description of techniques and treatments
- Average length of time to complete treatment

Massage Therapy

Massage therapists use strokes, kneading, and other movements on superficial layers of muscle to positively affect the health and well-being of their clients. It is one of the oldest forms of medicine, possibly dating back as far as 3000 B.C. Modern massage emerged in the 19th century when Swedish gymnast Henrik Ling developed the principles of Swedish massage.

Forty-three states and the District of Columbia have laws regulating massage therapy, and the National Certification Board for Therapeutic Massage and Bodywork certifies practitioners who pass a national examination. Many states that license massage therapists require them to pass a national exam, have a minimum of 500 hours of training at an accredited institution, meet specific continuing education requirements, and carry malpractice insurance.

How does massage therapy help? The skin is the body's largest organ, and it is "wired" for touch. Adults have about 20 square feet of skin with at least 5 million touch receptors. Touch is a critical human need and is as important for our development as food, clothing, and shelter. And it is the most intimate and powerful form of communication between two people. Massage is a strong, sustained touch. A skilled massage therapist loosens and gradually improves blood flow and the movement of lymph fluid throughout the body. Massage speeds up the movement of the body's waste products and allows more oxygen and nutrients to reach the tissues. It can stimulate the release of endorphins and brain chemicals.

Massage therapy may help relieve headaches, backaches, muscle pain, insomnia, anxiety, and depression, all of which can accompany PTSD. It has been used as an addition to conventional psychotherapy. Clients are usually given a chair massage: They are fully dressed and seated in a massage chair while the head, neck, arms, legs, and back are massaged for 10 to 20 minutes per session. Massage therapy relieves stress and is believed to help the body's stress response by lowering levels of stress hormones such as cortisol.

There are five basic techniques that are used in any style of massage therapy.

1. *Effleurage:* Long, firm strokes that are used at the beginning of a treatment to warm the superficial tissues.
2. *Petrissage:* Grasping, lifting, and stretching muscle groups then kneading them to help relieve the tissues of metabolic waste.
3. *Friction*: Using the fingers and thumbs to press on small areas and move in a circular motion around the area.
4. *Vibration*: Placing the hands on a muscle group and moving them back and forth quickly.
5. *Tapotement/percussion*: Striking the skin with the outside edges of the hands, fingers, or cupped palms to stimulate circulation.

Like any other treatment, massage therapy has side effects. People have experienced minor discomfort, bruising, or swelling after a massage. However, people have also reported unexpected positive side effects, including improved digestive or respiratory function.

Cautions with Massage Therapy

There are certain conditions that can make massage problematic. If you have any of these, condition, you *should not* have massage therapy:

- Fever
- Blood pressure problems

What Nurses Know...

Shiatsu massage is the Japanese version of acupressure. It may be beneficial for anxiety.

- Severe varicose veins
- Blood clots
- Inflammation of the skin, soft tissue, or joints
- Burns
- Bleeding or soft tissue damage
- Herniated disc
- Recent fractures or strains
- Some types of cancer
- Advanced osteoporosis
- Bleeding disorders
- Taking blood-thinning drugs

Hypnosis

Hypnosis, or hypnotherapy, creates a trance-like state in which people have heightened focus, concentration, and inner absorption. The trance state is induced by using guided imagery, relaxation, deep breathing, meditation techniques, self-hypnosis, or hypnosis induction techniques. Individuals vary in their ability to enter this state; however, most people gain some benefit from this therapy. When under hypnosis, people usually feel calm and relaxed. They are able to concentrate intensely on a specific thought, memory, feeling, or sensation while blocking out distractions, and they are more open to suggestions, although their free will remains intact and they do not lose control over their behavior. Hypnosis has been studied for a number of conditions,

What Nurses Know...

Hypnosis has been used to treat war-related trauma for a long time. Recently it has been used in cases of sexual assault, Holocaust survival, and car accidents. Hypnosis creates a deep state of relaxation, which may help people with PTSD feel safer and less anxious, decrease intrusive thoughts, and become involved in their daily activities again. It is usually used together with psychotherapy and requires a trained, licensed hypnotherapist.

including state anxiety (such as before surgery), smoking cessation, and pain control.

Hypnosis dates back to ancient religious practices and Eastern mystical experiences that involved similar trance states or altered states of consciousness. Experimentation with hypnosis has occupied an essential role in the early days of psychiatry and psychology. Since then, hypnosis has been incorporated into psychology and is now seen as an adjunct therapy.

Cautions with Hypnotherapy

When hypnosis is conducted by a trained therapist or health-care professional, it is considered a safe CAM treatment. Side effects are rare, but may include: headache, dizziness, nausea, anxiety, panic, and creation of false memories. However, to date there are no laws that limit the use of hypnotherapy to professionals; anyone can hypnotize. Therefore, it is critical that you find a hypnotist who is also a nurse, physician, psychologist, social worker, or counselor, so that person will know about both hypnosis and PTSD.

Homeopathy

Homeopathy is designed to utilize diluted preparations that mimic the symptoms that you are suffering from in order to treat your illness. It is the "hair of the dog that bit you." This practice, called "the law of similars," was developed by the founder of homeopathic medicine, German physician Samuel Hahnemann in 1796. According to homeopaths, the practice causes a curative response by stimulating the immune system. Specifically, the "cure" begins from the top of the body downward, and outward from internal to external as symptoms clear in the reverse order they presented. Before prescribing, homeopaths consider your constitutional type, which is your physical, emotional, and intellectual makeup. Homeopathy does not seek to suppress symptoms, but rather to recognize and remove underlying causes.

There is little research on the effectiveness of homeopathic remedies. However, homeopaths may be considered for treatment of PTSD based on their knowledge and experience. About half of the practicing homeopaths in the United States are physicians. The others are licensed healthcare providers, including nurse practitioners.

One of the homeopathic remedies used for PTSD is Arnica, an extract from sunflowers. Arnica is used for chronic conditions, such as depression, that can occur after a traumatic experience and is most appropriate for people who generally deny that anything is wrong. Arnica may decrease the effect of blood pressure medications and increase the effect of platelet drugs, and thus should be used with caution if you are taking these medications. It is also very toxic in children.

Cautions with Homeopathy

If you use homeopathic remedies, you may experience a brief increase of symptoms before your condition improves. Therefore, it is important to have a qualified support team in place to help you handle any worsening of symptoms.

What Nurses Know...

The Council of Homeopathic Certification certifies homeopaths using strict guidelines that include a specific number of training hours, three years of clinical practice, and written and oral examinations. Homeopaths certified by this organization use the letters "DHt" after their name.

Acupuncture

Acupuncture, which originated China, is one of the oldest healing practices in the world. It is based on the concept that disease results from disruption in the flow of energy, called qi or chi. Qi is thought to run along body pathways called meridians. Meridians act like electrical power lines and connect all the parts of the body. Energy flows through the meridians and form tiny points near the surface of the skin. Acupuncturists insert thin needles through the skin at specific points to remove blockages in the flow of qi to restore and maintain health.

Westernized medicine takes a more scientific approach to explaining how acupuncture works. They see acupuncture points as places to stimulate nerves, muscles, and other body tissue. This stimulation seems to boost the body's natural painkillers and increase blood flow.

What Nurses Know...

Acupressure works on the same principles as acupuncture. Instead of needles, practitioners use finger pressure on the specific points to remove the blockage of qi.

The U.S. Food and Drug Administration (FDA) regulates acupuncture needles for use by licensed practitioners. They require that needles are manufactured and labeled according to certain standards, and are sterile, nontoxic, and labeled for single use. When conducted by a qualified professional, there are relatively few side effects; however, when done by someone who is not qualified, potentially serious side effects, such as infections and punctured organs, can occur.

Cautions with Acupuncture

Not everyone is a good candidate for particular types of acupuncture. If you are considering having acupuncture, make sure to talk to your healthcare provider and to tell the acupuncturist about your general health problems. Certain conditions can result in complications:

- Avoid acupuncture if you have a bleeding disorder or are using blood thinning drugs such as Coumadin (warfarin).
- Avoid acupuncture if you have a pacemaker (some types of acupuncture involve applying mild electrical pulses to the needle).
- If you are pregnant, or if you have gallstones or kidney stones, be sure to discuss these conditions with your acupuncturist because certain stimulation points should be avoided.

Herbal Medicines

Many people who experience symptoms of anxiety do not seek medical attention. Instead, they turn to alternative treatments, especially herbal medicines. The use of these products is extremely common. Herbal medicine is used by 80% of the world's population, and they are the most popular alternative therapy in the United States. Have you ever had a cup of peppermint tea or a

What Nurses Know...

Natural does not mean safe. Herbs contain ingredients that can cause side effects or interact with other herbs or medications.

glass of ginger ale for an upset stomach? How about chamomile tea to help you sleep? If so, then you have used herbal medicine without even knowing it!

Herbal medicines are dietary supplements sold as tablets, capsules, powders, teas, extracts, and fresh or dried plants. People have been taking herbal medicines for ages to treat disease and improve their well-being. However, herbs contain components that can cause side effects and interact with other herbs, supplements, or medications. Therefore, herbs should be taken with care and under the supervision of your healthcare provider or preferably a professional qualified in the field of botanical medicine.

Herbal remedies used for anxiety include chamomile, kava kava, lavender, St. John's wort, and valerian.

CHAMOMILE

There are two types of chamomile used for health conditions, German chamomile and Roman chamomile. Their effects are similar, but the German variety is more common in the United States. Chamomile has been widely used for thousands of years for a variety of health conditions, including sleeplessness, anxiety, upset stomach, gas, and diarrhea. It is also used topically for skin problems and orally for mouth ulcers that result from cancer treatment.

Cautions with Chamomile

- Chamomile is widely available and widely used; however, there have been reports of allergic reactions including rashes and anaphylaxis, a life-threatening allergic reaction. If you are allergic to plants in the daisy family, which includes ragweed, chrysanthemums, marigolds, and daisies, you may be allergic to chamomile. Avoid it.
- If you have a bleeding disorder or are using blood thinners, talk to your healthcare provider before taking chamomile.
- Chamomile may cause depression. If you already have symptoms of depression, avoid using chamomile.
- Don't take chamomile if you have asthma because it may make your asthma worse.
- Don't take chamomile if you are pregnant because of a risk of miscarriage.
- Chamomile may cause problems when taken with certain other drugs, including sedatives. If you are taking other medications, talk to your healthcare provider before taking chamomile.

KAVA KAVA

Kava kava is a member of the pepper family and is said to improve your mood and well-being and produce a feeling of relaxation. It has been used for sleeplessness and fatigue, as well as for anxiety, insomnia, and menopausal symptoms. Research has provided some evidence that kava kava may be beneficial for the management of anxiety.

Cautions with Kava Kava

- The FDA has issued a warning that kava kava supplements are linked to a risk of severe liver damage. If you have any problems with your liver, don't take kava kava.
- Don't take kava kava if you are pregnant or breast feeding.
- Don't take kava kava if you are going to have surgery, and tell your surgeon if you have used kava kava in the past.

- Don't take kava kava if you have Parkinson's disease or if you have had a stroke.
- Don't take kava kava if you are taking an antianxiety medication, especially Xanax (alprazolam). It may also interact with certain antipsychotic medications, anticonvulsants, and diuretics.
- Don't use kava kava when also taking St. John's wort.
- If you are taking kava kava, don't use alcohol.
- Do not give kava kava to children.

LAVENDER

Lavender is used for anxiety, restlessness, insomnia, and depression, although there is little evidence for its effectiveness. Lavender is usually used in aromatherapy whereby the scent of its essential oils is inhaled to promote health and well-being. The oil can also be diluted and applied to the skin, and the dried lavender flowers can be used to make tea or liquid extracts.

Cautions with Lavender

- Topical lavender oil and lavender aromatherapy are generally considered safe for most adults, although the oil can cause skin irritation.
- Do not drink lavender oil; it may be poisonous.
- Lavender tea may cause headache, appetite changes, and constipation.
- Use lavender with caution if taking sedatives.

ST. JOHN'S WORT

St. John's wort has been used for centuries to treat mental disorders, and is used today by some people for depression, anxiety, and sleep disorders. There is evidence that St. John's wort may be useful in the short-term for mild and moderate depression; however, it is not a proven therapy for depression.

Cautions for St. John's Wort
- Side effects can include increased sensitivity to sunlight, anxiety, dry mouth, dizziness, gastrointestinal symptoms, fatigue, headache, or sexual dysfunction.
- St. John's wort also may interact with several medications. If you are on medication, talk to your healthcare provider before taking St. John's wort.
- If you are taking St. John's wort, avoid eating foods that contain tyramine; these include aged cheeses; some wines; cured meats, such as sausage, pepperoni, and salami; sauerkraut; soy sauce; fava beans; banana peels; and draft (tap) beer. The combination can cause dangerously high blood pressure.

VALERIAN

The therapeutic values of valerian were described by Hippocrates, and valerian is still used by people for anxiety and sleep disorders. The roots and underground stems of this plant are used to make capsules, tablets, and liquid extracts, as well as teas. Research suggests that valerian may be helpful for insomnia, but there is not enough evidence to confirm this, nor is there evidence to determine of it works for anxiety or depression.

Cautions with Valerian
- Valerian is generally safe to use for short periods of time, usually 4 to 6 weeks, but may cause mild side effects such as headaches, dizziness, upset stomach, and morning tiredness.
- Valerian may cause severe liver damage, so do not take it if you have any liver problems.
- Don't take with sedatives or antihistamines as the combination can cause severe sedation.
- If you take valerian, don't drink alcohol.

POSSIBLE HERBAL AND MEDICATION INTERACTIONS

Chamomile

- *Aspirin*
- *Platelet inhibitors, including Plavix (clopidogrel)*
- *Anticoagulants, including Coumadin (warfarin); tricyclic antidepressants, including Elavil (amitriptyline), Anafranil (clomipramine), Tofranil (imipramine), Clozaril (clozapine)*
- *Inderal (propranolol)*
- *Theolair, Slo-bid, Slo-Phyllin (theophylline)*
- *Cognex (tacrine)*

Kava Kava

- *Anticonvulsants*
- *Alcohol*
- *Anxiety agents*
- *Phenothiazine medications (chlorpromazine and promethazine)*
- *Levodopa*

Lavender

May increase the central nervous system depressant effects of sedative-hypnotic medications

St. John's Wort

- *Antidepressants*
- *Birth control pills*
- *Cyclosporine, which prevents the body from rejecting transplanted organs*
- *Digoxin, a heart medication*
- *Indinavir and possibly other drugs used to control HIV infection*
- *Irinotecan and possibly other drugs used to treat cancer*

- *Seizure-control drugs, such as dilantin and phenobarbital*
- *Warfarin and related anticoagulants.*

Valerian

- *Alcohol*
- *Xanax (alprazolam)*
- *Sedative medications (benzodiazepines)*
- *Medications changed by the liver (cytochrome P450 3A4 [CYP3A4] substrates)*

Partners: Helping Your Healthcare Providers Help You

"Eventual salvation: Finally telling someone in my 30s and getting into therapy. As an adult, developing a relationship with dogs—pure, simple, accepting, undemanding creatures who love us no matter how awful our self-perception. Dogs were (and still are) the agents of bringing light to my soul. It took many years and many dogs. Finally living a life of joy and finding validation in service to other abused victims, notably emotionally disturbed children in special ed. I am not only a survivor; I am a thrivor (to coin a word)." ABBY

The first, and most important, step in getting help is recognizing that a problem exists. PTSD affects you and your family. If your symptoms are interfere significantly with your relationships, job, or any other important part of your life, it is time to get professional help. Everyone needs mentors on their journeys. Luke Skywalker had Obi Wan Kenobi; the Karate Kid had Mr. Miyagi; you have your healthcare provider and therapist.

Finding a Primary Care Provider

If you already have a primary care provider (PCP), you can skip this section. However, if you are like many other adults who rely on emergency departments and urgent care centers for your healthcare, you may want to consider finding a PCP for your routine health care, especially since your PTSD may be associated with stress-related physical health problems.

PCPs see people who have common medical problems. This healthcare provider may be a physician, but may also be a nurse practitioner (NP) or physician assistant (PA). Most people keep their PCP for a long time, so it is important to select someone with whom you will work well. Your PCP will:

- Provide you with preventive care
- Teach you healthy lifestyle choices
- Identify and treat common medical conditions
- Make referrals to medical specialists when necessary
- Depending on the circumstances, direct or assist in your care if you are admitted to the hospital

There are many different types of PCPs:

- **Family practitioners** are physicians who have completed medical school and a family practice residency. They are usually board certified for family practice by the American Board of Family Medicine. Family physicians care for children and adults, and some also do obstetrics and minor surgeries.
- **Internists** are physicians who have completed medical school and a residency in internal medicine. They are usually board certified for internal medicine by the American Board of

What Nurses Know...

Board certification is different than licensing. All primary care providers need to be licensed in the state where they practice. Board certified means that the primary healthcare provider has also met specific qualifications (usually education, experience, and passing an exam) to practice their specialty. There are different professional boards that certify specific professions.

Internal Medicine. They care for adults of all ages for many different medical problems. Internists have special training in working with persons who have complex, chronic illnesses, as well as those who have multiples illnesses.

- **Obstetricians/gynecologists** are physicians who have completed medical school and are board certified in their field by the American Board of Obstetrics and Gynecology. They manage pregnancy, labor, and the puerperium (the time period directly following childbirth), as well as female reproductive system disorders and diseases. They often serve as PCPs for women, particularly those of childbearing age.

- **Nurse practitioners** (NP) are registered nurses with advanced education (master's or doctoral degrees) and clinical experience. They provide a wide range of preventive and acute healthcare services to individuals of all ages, depending upon the nature of their advanced education. Primary care nurse practitioners care for children and adults (Family Nurse Practitioners), children/adolescents (Pediatric Nurse Practitioners), adults and older adults (Adult/Geriatric Nurse Practitioners), or women (Women's Health Nurse Practitioners). Most are nationally certified in their specialty area. There are different organizations for board certification for nurse practitioners; one of them is the American Nurses Credentialing Association.

- **Nurse midwives** (CNM) are registered nurses with advanced education and clinical experience who provide prenatal, labor and delivery, and afterbirth care, as well as primary healthcare for women of all ages. They are usually certified by the American Midwifery Certification Board.
- **Physician assistants** (PAs) practice medicine as members of a team with their supervising physicians. PAs deliver a broad range of medical and surgical services to diverse populations. They are usually certified by the National Commission on Certification of Physician Assistants.

One of the best ways to find a PCP is by asking family members, friends, or neighbors, as well as your dentist, pharmacist, or optometrist. You may also want to do an Internet search to check the "ratings" of a particular PCP, but remember that ratings are subjective and you don't know who wrote them. You can check

What Nurses Know...

Nurse practitioners (NPs) have been providing quality care for patients in a variety of settings since 1965. NPs practice within the scope of their state's nurse practice act and provide comprehensive care within an area of specialization and can: evaluate a person's health by taking a history, perform a physical examination; order and interprete results from laboratory and diagnostic tests/procedures; diagnose health and medical conditions; manage health problems; prescribe medications or treatments; obtain consultations and referrals; coordinate healthcare services; teach and counsel individuals, families, and groups; and collaborate with other healthcare providers.

with local or state medical, nursing, or physician assistant associations or check with your insurance company. You will need to make sure that your insurance plan covers your chosen provider. Many insurance plans limit the providers you can choose from, or provide incentives for you to select from their specific list of providers. You should also make sure you know what your insurance covers before starting to narrow down your options.

Once you narrow down your choice, set up an interview. When choosing a PCP, consider asking these questions:

- Is the office location convenient?
- Is there adequate parking?
- Is the PCP board certified?
- Do they have convenient office hours?
- How far in advance do you need to make appointments?
- How do they handle emergent and urgent problems?
- Who takes care of patients when the PCP is away?
- Is the office staff friendly and helpful?
- Is the office good about returning calls?
- Are the office hours convenient to your schedule?
- How easy is it to reach the provider?
- Does the provider use email?
- Do you prefer a provider whose communication style is friendly and warm, or more formal?
- Do you prefer a provider focused on disease treatment, or wellness and prevention?
- Does the provider have a conservative or aggressive approach to treatment?
- Does the provider order a lot of tests?
- Does the provider refer to other specialists frequently or infrequently?
- What do colleagues and patients say about the provider?
- Does the provider invite you to be involved in your care?
- Does the provider view your patient-doctor relationship as a true partnership?

What Nurses Know...

For more information on primary care providers, contact:
American Academy of Family Physicians
www.aafp.org
American Society of Internal Medicine
www.acponline.org
American College of Obstetricians and Gynecologists
www.acog.org
American College of Nurse Practitioners
www.acnpweb.org
American College of Nurse Midwives
www.midwife.org
American Academy of Physician Assistants
www.aapa.org

Talking to Your Primary Healthcare Provider

Gone are the days where your healthcare provider had plenty of time to ask you questions about how things are going in your and your family's lives. Today, healthcare offices are hectic places where patients move in and out at a rapid pace. Thus, you and your healthcare provider need to form a partnership based on trust and clear communications.

Make a list of what you want to discuss. You use lists to grocery shop, so why not use them for your health care? You can use the PTSD Health Care Checklist in this chapter to guide you. If you have other items to discuss, put them in order and ask about the most important ones first. Don't put off the things that are really on your mind until the end of your appointment–bring them up right away! If this is your first visit, go early so you can fill out any necessary forms.

THE PTSD HEALTHCARE CHECKLIST

Use this checklist to write down the information you need for your first healthcare and therapy visit. Take the information with you when you first talk to your primary healthcare provider and your therapist about your PTSD symptoms. They will ask you for more information, but by using this checklist, you will be able to discuss the important issues related to your PTSD without forgetting any of them.

Your insurance information: *Unfortunately, this tends to be one of the first things that they ask for.*

Triggering event: *Be prepared to tell your primary health-care provider or therapist as much as you can (and are comfortable with). They will want to assess the nature, severity, and duration of the trauma. They will also want to know when it happened.*

Your symptoms:

_____ *Recurrent and intrusive distressing memories of the trauma*

_____ *Recurrent distressing dreams of the trauma*

_____ *Acting as if the trauma was recurring:*

    _____ *Sense of reliving the experience*

    _____ *Illusions (distorted perception of something you actually see, like seeing a branch on the road at night while driving, but thinking it is a dog)*

    _____ *Hallucinations (seeing, hearing, feeling, tasting, or smelling something that is not really there)*

    _____ *Flashbacks (feeling you are back in the trauma)*

_____ *Intense distress when exposed to reminders that resemble or symbolize the trauma*

_____ *Efforts to avoid thoughts, feelings, or conversations associated with the trauma*

_____ *Efforts to avoid people, places, or activities associated with the trauma*

_____ *Inability to remember important aspects of the trauma*

_____ *Severely decreased interest or participation in significant activities*

_____ *Feeling detached or estranged from others*

_____ *Restricted range of feelings*

_____ *Sense of a shortened future*

_____ *Irritability or outbursts of anger*

_____ *Difficulty concentrating*

_____ *Hypervigilance*

_____ *Exaggerated startle response*

_____ *Other symptoms*

Your current health problems: *Any illnesses that you may have, such as heart disease, thyroid disease, nervous system problems, etc., including any mental health or substance abuse problems.*

Your past health problems: *Any significant illnesses, injuries, surgeries, and hospitalizations that you had in the past since childhood.*

Your medications: *Remember to include: prescription medicines, over-the-counter medications, birth control pills and devices, vitamins and supplements, herbal medicines, and home remedies. Write down the medication name, how often you take it, how much you take, and why you take it. If you take multiple medications, you may want to put them all in a bag and bring them with you.*

Mental health treatment: *Any mental health or substance abuse treatment you have received: medications, individual therapy, family therapy, group therapy, etc.*

Your habits: *This would include nicotine, alcohol and drug use, as well as your work, school, and leisure activities.*

Your relationships: *This includes your relationship with your spouse/partner, children, other family members, friends, and co-workers.*

Your family health problems: *Include chronic illnesses such as diabetes and heart disease, cancer, infectious diseases, mental illnesses, and drug or alcohol problems.*

Finding a Therapist

The ease of obtaining help depends on your location. Cities tend to have more therapists than rural areas. The types of therapists vary, both in educational background and specialty area. Many therapists specialize in areas such as family therapy or marital therapy. If at all possible, choose a therapist who specializes in PTSD or anxiety disorders in general. And, as with your primary care provider, chose a therapist who is board certified. Therapists include:

- *Psychiatrists* are physicians. After attending medical school and earning their MD, they go on to additional years of residency training in mental health, typically in a hospital's psychiatric department. Psychiatrists do conduct assessments and provide therapy, but psychiatrists can also order diagnostics tests, such as blood work, and they can prescribe medications.

- *Psychologists* usually complete five to seven years of academic graduate study, culminating in a doctorate degree. They may have PhD or a PsyD after their name. Those who are mainly interested in treating patients as opposed to focusing on research may pursue a PsyD. Licensing requirements vary from state to state, but at least a one- or two-year internship is usually required to apply for a license to practice psychology. In addition to psychotherapy and research, psychologists use a variety of psychological tests to examine a person's psychological issues. Some states have granted prescribing privileges to psychologists.

- *Psychiatric Nurse Practitioners* and *Psychiatric Clinical Nurse Specialists* are both registered nurses with graduate level education, either at the master's or doctoral level, who assess and treat individuals, families, and groups. Those with doctoral degrees will usually have DNP or PhD after their names. Both are educated to diagnose and treat; however, psychiatric nurse practitioners have prescriptive privileges in more states than do psychiatric clinical nurse specialists. Many psychiatric nurse practitioners focus on medication management, while psychiatric clinical nurse specialists focus on therapy.

- *Clinical social workers* (also called psychiatric social workers or mental health social workers) address the needs of individuals, families, couples, and groups affected by life changes and challenges, including mental disorders and other behavioral problems. A master's degree in social work (MSW) is typically required for social workers seeking positions in mental health fields. Social workers must also adhere to certification, licensing, and registration laws in their state.

If you don't know any therapists, try the following:

- Ask your family members or friends who have had experience with psychiatric treatment.

- Talk to your primary healthcare provider.
- Ask your Employee Assistance Program (EAP) personnel.
- Contact your local Mental Health Association or Medical Society. Both are listed in the white pages of your phone book. The Mental Health Association usually can be found under that listing, while the Medical Society is typically listed by county, for example, the Lackawanna County Medical Society.
- Contact your State American Psychological Association by calling the national number, 1-800-964-2000, visit their national web site (www.apa.org/helpcenter) or use their online psychologist locator (http://locator.apa.org).
- Call the American Psychiatric Nurses Association at 866.243.2443 or at www.apna.org
- Contact the National Association of Social Workers at www.socialworkers.org
- Contact the nearest college or university and speak to someone in their psychology, counseling, social work, or nursing program. Some colleges have faculty student practice centers that provide therapy at reasonable cost; others can help you with a referral.
- Check the yellow or blue pages of your phone book. This is the least effective method as you cannot determine the quality of care that you will receive.
- Utilize HelpPro at www.helppro.com

Once you have the names of one or more therapists, call and ask the following questions:

- Are you licensed and nationally certified?
- How long have you been in practice?
- How long have you worked with clients with PTSD?
- Do you specialize in PTSD or anxiety disorders?
- What are your fees? Do you accept my HMO or insurance coverage?

If you are unsure as to whether your insurance or HMO covers psychiatric treatment, call them and ask. Many cover some level of treatment, but insurance and HMO plans vary, so you need to find out about your coverage. Find out exactly what is covered and how long you will be covered. Ask if it covers all or part of the treatment, and if there are any limits, such as a limit on the number of visits, annual or lifetime maximums, or co-payments. Find out if your plan covers only "medically necessary" treatments, and, if so, what criteria they use to make that decision. Finally, make sure your plan covers the specific therapist that you choose as some have limitations on this. Find out what licenses, certifications, and degrees the therapist must have in order for reimbursement to be authorized.

Government programs such as Medicaid and CHAMPUS also provide varying levels of coverage. However, if you do not have coverage, ask the therapist if he or she has a sliding-scale fee or if you can work out a payment plan. If not, contact your Community Mental Health program to see one of their therapists.

What to Expect from Your Therapist

Therapy types vary, so ask your therapist what kind of treatment he/she uses, if this method would be effective for your PTSD symptoms, and for an estimate of how long therapy will last. Regardless of the therapist used, most adhere to the following.

- Therapists must guarantee strict confidentiality. Typically you must even sign a release form for your therapist to send information to your insurance company and even your primary healthcare provider.
- Therapists obtain a complete history, which may take several hours or visits to complete. With your permission, other people may be interviewed, such as your primary healthcare provider. The history usually includes:
  - A description of your PTSD symptoms

What Nurses Know...

Conversations with your therapist are confidential. However, there are certain situations when your therapist is obligated by law to break confidentiality and talk to the appropriate authorities:

- *If you threatened to harm or kill yourself*
- *If you threaten to harm or kill someone else*
- *If you admit to abusing a child or vulnerable adult (an elder, a hospitalized person, or a person with a disability)*

- General information about your present and past health, both physical and psychiatric
- Details about your family relationships
- Information about your relationship with friends
- Information about your activities (hobbies, substance use, etc.)
- Psychiatrists and nurse practitioners may order laboratory tests, such as blood tests and x-rays. Psychologists may conduct psychological testing.
- Some therapists will order or conduct special assessments such as psychological evaluations.
- Once the therapist gathers information, he or she will develop a plan to address your specific needs. The recommendations will include the suggestion of hospital or outpatient therapy. Most PTSD symptoms are managed on an outpatient basis.

Therapy itself refers to a variety of techniques and methods used to help you when you experience problems with emotions and behaviors. Each type of therapy relies on communication to bring about change in your feelings and actions. Therapy may involve individual sessions, family sessions, or group sessions with other people who have PTSD. Your PTSD symptoms may also warrant medication. Descriptions of therapies and medications can be found in Chapter 5.

Working with Your Therapist

For therapy to work, you need to feel understood and well supported by your therapist. Your therapist will use his or her skills to help you with the healing process. However, for therapy to work, you have to act as a team—you have to do your part, too. The first thing you need to do is realize that your therapist is a therapist, not a psychic. Your therapist cannot read your mind and automatically know how you think and feel. You need to tell your therapist. Therapists are not all-wise and all knowing, and they cannot just take care of everything. You will have to develop skills to manage your symptoms. It does require some work, but it's worth it. However, you are the consumer, so if things are not going well in therapy, tell your therapist. He or she can work with you to change your treatment plan so you get back on track. If your therapist cannot work with your needs, or if you are not comfortable with him or her, get another therapist.

As a partner in your treatment, there are many things you can do to get the most out of your therapy:

- Work with your therapist to set realistic treatment goals. If you set goals that you can't reach, you'll get frustrated and want to quit altogether.
- Keep your appointments. If you miss one, you may be tempted to miss more.
- Follow your treatment plan. If something is not working, don't ignore it; talk to your therapist about changing the plan.
- Be honest. Share your thoughts, feelings, and experiences with your therapist. If you can't talk about a specific feeling or event, tell your therapist. Your therapist will help you ease into talking about it over time.

- Be open to change. You need new ways to deal with your symptoms.
- Do your homework. Many therapists, especially those using cognitive behavioral therapy, want you to work on your new skills between sessions.
- Think positively. This may be difficult, especially if you are feeling depressed. But thinking negatively will only hold you back. You need to move forward, so think positively!

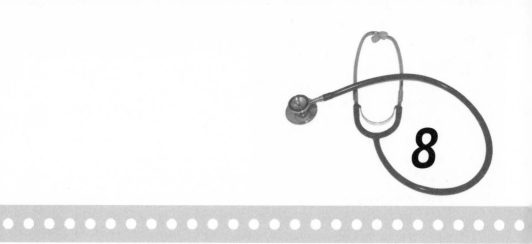

8

Stress: The Good, the Bad, and Dealing with All of It

"It wasn't over for my young sisters, though, even though my mother knew and did nothing to protect them. My young sister, who was born when I was away at college, was abused for years by my father and eventually hanged herself at the age of 25. I found her body and the note she left. It was unimaginable. I will carry the guilt for not helping my younger sisters to my grave. As I said, I was a fool to believe my mother." ABBY

Stress is an epidemic. Findings from the 2010 American Psychological Association Stress in America show the United States as an overstressed nation. The effects of prolonged financial and other recession-related difficulties cause Americans to struggle to balance work and home life with making time to engage in healthy behaviors. Stress not only takes a toll on Americans personal physical health, it also affects the emotional and physical well-being of their families. Americans recognize that their stress levels exceed what they consider to be healthy. We understand the importance of healthy behaviors, but we report experiencing challenges practicing these healthy behaviors, primarily because we're too busy to manage our stress, as well as our lack of motivation, energy, and time.

Stress is a natural bodily function in response to a real or perceived threat, leading to quick reaction—fight or flight. Any disrupting activity or event can be stressful—traffic jams, waiting in lines, juggling career and family, even positive events such as graduations, weddings, and the birth of a child. Whatever the trigger, a cascade of physical and emotional responses follows.

The nervous and endocrine systems are responsible for the body's physical response to stress. The autonomic nervous system contains two parts, the parasympathetic and sympathetic divisions. The parasympathetic division is in charge while you are relaxed, controlling digestion, breathing, heart rate, blood pressure, and hundreds of other activities. The sympathetic division activates during emergencies and targets several organs including blood vessels, muscles, and sweat glands. The sympathetic system commands your body to stop storing energy and to start using it in response to stressors.

What Nurses Know...

Stress is nothing new, but contemporary stress tends to be more pervasive, persistent, and insidious because it comes from both psychological and physical threats.

Thus, digestion stops, hearing increases, the bladder empties to release excess weight, the pupils dilate to better vision, the heart accelerates to increase blood flow to where it's needed, voluntary muscles contract to ready for action, and the adrenal glands stimulate secretion of adrenaline (the "fear hormone") and noradrenaline (the "anger hormone") to create changes that boost energy.

Emotional responses to stress vary from person to person. Some people respond well to stressors by talking, laughing, exercising, meditating, or problem solving. Others respond poorly by developing physical symptoms or by reacting inappropriately and using such behaviors as aggressively acting-out or using substances.

Signs of Stress

Stress overload can challenge your ability to care for yourself, your family, and your job. It can also cause stress-related disorders, encompass a broad array of conditions, including:

- Psychological disorders (depression, anxiety, PTSD)
- Emotional distress (job dissatisfaction, fatigue, tension)
- Maladaptive behaviors (aggression, substance abuse)
- Cognitive impairment (concentration and memory problems)

These conditions can lead to poor work performance or even injury, as well as various biological reactions that may lead ultimately to compromised health, such as cardiovascular disease. Stress is also expensive. High levels of stress are associated with substantial increases in health service utilization, longer disability periods for occupational injuries and illnesses, and major staff turnover in organizations.

Chronic stress leads to feelings of being "stressed out" or "burned out." Stress may not be easy to recognize because it often affects the body, leading one to believe that they are ill rather than stressed out. Signs of chronic stress include:

- Headaches, backaches, chest pain, stomachaches, indigestion, nausea, or diarrhea
- Rashes
- Overeating or undereating
- Sleep disturbances (too much sleep, restless sleep, difficulty falling asleep, difficulty staying asleep, waking up early)
- Fatigue
- Disillusionment
- Sexual dysfunction
- Workaholic behavior and/or continuously thinking about work
- Twitching
- Having trouble concentrating or with school work
- Breakdown of personal relationships
- Feeling anxious or worried
- Feeling inadequate, frustrated, helpless, or overwhelmed
- Feeling bored or dissatisfied
- Feeling pressured, tense, irritable, angry, or hostile
- Aggressive behavior
- Substance abuse
- Excessive or inappropriate crying
- Avoiding others
- Mood swings
- Inability to organize or make decisions
- Blocked creativity or judgment
- Poor memory/ forgetfulness
- Difficulty concentrating

Physiologic Effects of Stress

Stress can cause an array of physiological problems that range from headache, upset stomach, muscular tension, and tightness in the chest to cardiac and immunological diseases. The hormones released during the alarm phase of the stress reaction can be protective, but they can also promote organ damage and accelerate pathologic changes that lead to many common ailments and diseases if not abated over time. The disease of adaptation syndrome is a set of adverse physiologic changes that occur when the body is so overwhelmed by a stressor that it can no longer maintain homeostasis and ultimately becomes exhausted.

CARDIOVASCULAR EFFECTS

People who are prone to frequent and big increases in their blood pressure during stress are believed to be at risk for developing hypertension, stroke, and fatty deposits in the blood vessels of the heart. Experts still are not sure how stress increases the risk of heart disease. Stress might be a risk factor, but it could be that high levels of stress make other risk factors, such as high cholesterol, worse. When under stress, your blood pressure goes up, and you may exercise less, eat more, and may smoke.

What Nurses Know...

American Heart Association Warning Signs of a Heart Attack

- Discomfort in the center of the chest that lasts more than a few minutes, or that goes away and comes back. The pain can feel like uncomfortable pressure, squeezing, fullness or pain.
- Additional discomfort includes pain or discomfort in one or both arms, the back, neck, jaw, or stomach.
- Shortness of breath with or without chest discomfort.
- Breaking out in a cold sweat, nausea, or lightheadedness.

If stress itself is a risk factor, it could be because chronic stress exposes your body to unhealthy, persistently elevated levels of stress hormones like adrenaline and cortisol. Some studies also link stress to how the blood clots, which increases the risk of heart attack.

METABOLIC SYNDROME

Metabolic syndrome, a problem that is believed to affect 47 million people in the United States, is the term used for a combination of disorders that increase a person's risk for developing cardiovascular disease and Type 2 diabetes. The features of this syndrome include a combination of impaired sugar and fat metabolism, obesity, and hypertension. The professional literature suggests that psychological attributes and stressful events may predict the incidence of cardiovascular disease and Type 2 diabetes. Researchers found that depressive symptoms, very stressful life events, frequent and intense feelings of anger and tension, and stress are associated with the cumulative prevalence and risk for developing the metabolic syndrome in healthy, middle-age women.

What Nurses Know...

Symptoms of Metabolic Syndrome
- *Obesity, especially around your waist (apple shape).*
- *Systolic (top number) blood pressure measurement higher than 120 or a diastolic (bottom number) blood pressure measurement higher than 80.*
- *Elevated triglycerides with a low level of high-density lipoprotein (HDL) cholesterol, the "good" cholesterol.*
- *Insulin resistance.*

IMMUNE SYSTEM

Chronic stress suppresses your immune system and makes you vulnerable to illness and disease. When your immune system is dysfunctional it leaves your body vulnerable to infections, allergies, and perhaps cancer. If you already have a chronic immune problem, such as HIV disease, chronic stress can make it worse.

PEPTIC ULCER DISEASE

Stress does not cause ulcers, but it can make them worse. The exact association between stress and ulcers remains unclear, but several theories have been proposed. First, high levels of stress may increase a person's smoking, alcohol ingestion, and non-steroidal anti-inflammatory drug (e.g., ibuprophen) use and decrease sleep. These activities might lower mucosal defenses in the stomach, which lead to peptic ulcers. A second theory is that stress negatively alters physiologic mechanisms, increasing gastric acid secretion and lowering immunologic defenses, leading to a higher duodenal acid load and making a person more susceptible to duodenal ulcers. These changes can also increase susceptibility to *Helicobacter pylori* infection, a possible factor in peptic ulcer disease.

INFERTILITY

Stress reduces the probability of conceiving in a menstrual cycle, increases the risk of early pregnancy loss, and may lead to infertility. Infertility treatments can cause additional emotional stress and can increase the number of unsuccessful treatments. About 15% to 20% of infertile couples experience such significant emotional distress that they need psychological counseling. Whether infertility causes stress or if stressors cause infertility is yet to be determined; however, infertility and its treatment can be stressful, warranting stress management techniques.

Managing Stress

The effects of stress disorders can be devastating; however, you can actively avoid these pitfalls.

PERSONAL STRESS MANAGEMENT

Stress overload can impair overall functioning. Don't make major life decisions (job changes, divorce, relocations) while stressed, and don't make major purchases while stressed, which may cause temporary relief but long-term stress if you cannot afford them. Here are some tips to manage stress in your everyday life:

- Practice what you preach.
- Maintain boundaries, including those between work and home life.
- Take time for yourself with time-outs and leisure activities.
- Make time for family and friends.
- Use humor—laughter is the best medicine.
- Eat right, exercise regularly, and get enough sleep.
- Discontinue or minimize your use of caffeine.
- Use time management techniques:
  - Keep a calendar and be sure to block out time for those things that always go wrong but are out of your hands.
  - Plan ahead.
  - Prioritize.
  - Create to-do lists, but always have one thing already done, so you can scratch it off.
  - Do not over commit yourself—learn how to say no.
  - Delegate—give your kids chores to both decrease your stress and to increase their sense of responsibility.
  - Limit distractions and don't procrastinate.
- Try meditation or relaxation exercises.
- Delegate—rely on team work and do not do it all yourself.

- Stop being a perfectionist.
- Debrief—have family meetings to talk about household stressors (but don't overload the children with the adult stress issues, such as financial difficulties).

You can also try the ABC approach to decreasing one's risk of secondary trauma.

AWARENESS, BALANCE, AND CONNECTION

Awareness

- Be aware of your "trauma map." Acknowledge your past and be aware that it can affect how you view and perform.
- Inventory your current lifestyle choices and make necessary changes—are you eating, sleeping, and exercising adequately?
- Take care of yourself. Make a self-care list and post it prominently in your home or office. Include some of the following:
  - Be creative
  - Get away
  - Get outside and appreciate the weather
  - Enjoy other environments
  - Have fun
  - Socialize

Balance

- Allow yourself to fully experience emotional reactions. Don't keep your emotions "bottled up."
- Avoid working overtime and don't spend all of your free time socializing only with coworkers, discussing the negative factors of your job.
- Know your limits and accept them. Set realistic goals.
- Practice time management skills to help achieve a sense of balance in both your professional and personal lives.
- Seek out a new leisure activity unrelated to your job.

- Recognize negative coping skills, avoid them and substitute these coping skills with the more positive coping skills.

Connection

- Listen to feedback from colleagues, friends, and family members, and encourage at least one of them to conduct periodic "pulse checks."
- Avoid isolation and remain connected with and supported by your coworkers on the job -just don't spend all your time with them.
- Develop support systems with an informal peer support group, or seek out or become a mentor. Helping others is a great way to help yourself.
- Nurture your spiritual side.

WORK STRESS MANAGEMENT

Institutions benefit greatly when they keep stress levels to a minimum; employees are more productive and clients are more satisfied. Administrators can start by being positive role models, managing their own stress at home and work. See if your job participates in the following:

- Educating employees about job stress
- Minimizing stressors, including work overload, inadequate work space, insufficient resources, and unsafe equipment and situations
- Holding regular staff meetings, keeping the lines of communication open, and providing support
- Providing regular debriefing meetings
- Maintaining an organized and efficient workplace
- Taking action on legitimate complaints
- Providing readily available counseling

Employers usually have programs that address workplace stress, such as Employee Assistance Programs (EAP). EAPs can improve the ability of workers to cope with difficult work situations. Stress management programs teach workers about the nature and sources of stress, the effects of stress on health, and personal skills to reduce it. Check with your job to see if it has an EAP. If so, contact them to see if they have any programs for stress management.

Spirituality and Purpose

Spiritual wellness entails the capacity for compassion, love, altruism, forgiveness, joy, and fulfillment. It is the antidote to fear, anxiety, self-absorption, anger, cynicism, and pessimism. Spirituality transcends individuals to become a common bond between people. Some people look to organized religions to develop spiritual health, while others find meaning and purpose in their lives on their own through meditation, nature, art, or good works.

SPIRITUAL DISTRESS

Spiritual distress involves disruption in the life principle that pervades a person's entire being. It may be related to the inability to practice spiritual rituals, a conflict between spiritual beliefs and other aspects of life, or the crisis of illness, suffering, or death. Other definitions identify spiritual distress with unmet desires for support, compassion, and knowledgeable caring, as well as unmet needs for forgiveness, love, hope, and trust, and an individual's inability to reach beyond the concerns of the self.

Some people have been seriously harmed by their religious communities. They were shunned or excommunicated or told that they were evil. Some were forced into a rigidly controlled lifestyle by members of cults. Still others were physically or sexually abused. These people may feel that God has abandoned them, or that the idea of God is foolish or even destructive.

What Nurses Know...

The Survivors Network of Those Abused by Priests (SNAP) is the largest and most active support group for women and men wounded by religious authority figures. To contact them, call their toll-free phone number: 1-877-SNAPHEALS (1-877-762-7432) or visit their website at: www.snapnetwork.org

THE NATURE OF SPIRITUALITY

Spirituality goes beyond religious affiliation, striving for inspiration, reverence, meaning, purpose, and a sense of awe, even for those who do not believe in God. Spirituality tries to be in harmony with the universe, strives for answers about the infinite, and comes to focus when people face stress, illness, and death. All people have spirituality within them, but not all have the same depth or intensity. Deeply spiritual people feel that they are not alone in times of crisis, whereas those with little spirituality may feel alone and hopeless, without purpose or meaning in their lives. Victor Frankel, author of *Man's Search for Meaning*, states that when life has no meaning, it becomes empty, an "existential vacuum," which is a state of inertia, boredom, and apathy. If this state persists, it progresses into existential frustration, and people try to fill their existential vacuum with drugs, violence, food, overwork, and other such activities, yet remain unfulfilled.

The chief characteristics of spirituality include a sense of wholeness and harmony with one's self and others, and with a higher power. People experience and project strong identity, personal security, and a sense of hope. This does not mean that these individuals feel totally satisfied with life or that they know all the answers. Everyone has times of anxiety, helplessness, and confusion. These difficult situations generate spiritual questions and help people realize that their spirituality is valid, characterized by:

- *Holism.* Holism perceives the universe as a system of harmonious interconnectedness rather than the just sum of its parts, integrating body, mind, and spirit.
- *Faith.* Spirituality is easily identified in people who have faith and belief in the power and presence of a higher power in their lives. Faith enables them to believe that God helps them in their times of trouble, sorrow, and pain, and that He will never forget or abandon them in their time of need. Some researchers believe that faith can increase the body's resistance to stress.
- *Hope.* Spirituality is easily identified in those who have hope and trust in God's mercy, wisdom, and justice. Their hope enables them to hand problems and stressors over to God's hands. Without hope, the positive attitude that a person assumes in the face of difficulty, people can become depressed and more prone to illness.
- *Love.* Spiritual people actively show love, concern, and generosity to others. They're altruistic and giving, making a difference in people's lives. A close network of supportive family and friends can offer protection against many diseases. Research shows that people who experience love and support tend to resist unhealthy behaviors and feel less stressed.
- *Forgiveness.* Forgiveness is a release of hostility and resentment from past hurts. This doesn't mean that the person forgets the event. Instead it means that they let go of any revenge fantasies, resentment, or bitterness against the person that caused the harm. A Stanford University study found that college students trained to forgive were significantly less angry, more hopeful, and better able to deal with emotions than students not trained to forgive. Forgiveness frees up a great deal of energy that can be used in more positive manners.

- *Spiritual Need.* Spiritual need represents the person's need for meaning in all experiences and a dynamic relationship with self, others, and the Supreme Being. People derive their spiritual needs through affective experiences of faith, hope, and love—needs that include trust, relatedness, creativity, and grace.
- *Spiritual Quest.* Life can be viewed as a spiritual quest to answer life's questions and to seek a higher level of consciousness. Frankel spoke of the quest for meaning in one's life, stating that we search for meaning through creativity, relationships, and unavoidable suffering.
- *Spiritual Well-Being.* Spiritual well-being defines an affirmation of life, peace, harmony, and a sense of interconnectedness with God, self, community, and nature. Harmony and interconnectedness are the two major determinants of spiritual well-being in those who are healthy, as well as those who are terminally ill.

SPIRITUAL VALUES, BELIEFS, CUSTOMS, AND TRADITIONS

Customs build on beliefs, and beliefs build on values. Many people are unaware of their values, even though they can express them through their beliefs and customs. People acquire their values early in childhood, and these values guide their aspirations, goals, and behaviors.

Beliefs include opinions, knowledge, and faith about the world. Beliefs can range from atheism (belief that there is no God) to agnosticism (belief that God's existence is unknown or unknowable) to theism (belief that God is perfect and the creator of the universe). Beliefs, faiths, and values interconnect—what one sets one's heart on, believes in, or lives out is what one values.

Customs are learned behaviors visible through observation. Expressions of spirituality tend to follow an established order of practices, usually through a specific religious group. Practices range from simple meditation and relaxation to church services and rituals at shrines. Many observances take place at home, in private with the family. Some traditions involve special foods or ceremonies on specific holy days, and these celebrations hold symbolic meaning and a deep sense of miracle to those who follow the practices. Most religions have rituals to celebrate life stages, such as birth, entrance into adulthood, and death.

Some people practice their spirituality daily, while others only practice it on holy days. Regardless of the beliefs a person holds or the frequency of practice, beliefs fulfill certain needs:

- Give meaning to life, crises, and death
- Contribute a sense of security
- Guide everyday habits
- Drive acceptance or rejection of others
- Furnish psychological support
- Provide strength
- Offer healing

NURTURING SPIRITUALITY

By nurturing your spirituality, you develop your sense of personal value, sense of belonging in the world, and belief that you have the capacity for joy and fulfillment. To nurture your spirituality:

- Model your spiritual self.
- Recognize the spiritual reality in everyday life—the blueness of the sky, a cold glass of water, the change of the seasons.
- Live your values: sharing, thankfulness, trust, sacrifice, honor, faith, hope, and love.
- Encourage quiet reflection time, especially at night to give yourself a chance to reflect upon your day.
- Share words of love and acceptance.

- Pray together with your family. Shared prayer is one of the most intimate and deepest forms of communication.
- Show respect for all family members and others.
- As your children grow, help them negotiate between the dominant American culture and the countervailing values of the communities of faith.
- Foster a sense of community by volunteering with your children. Even small children can participate by donating old toys and clothes to children in need.
- Engage in your faith together. Actively participate in religious functions, holidays, and rituals, and explain their meaning to your children.
- Make each day a new beginning. It's not the end of the world if you lose your temper or make a mistake. Start over. Forgiveness and faith means knowing that spirituality moves and breathes and is our life force.

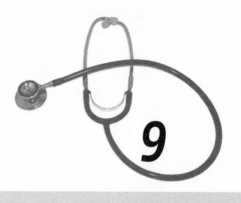

9

Broken Bonds: When Your Partner Has PTSD

Bye, Bye Soldier
The sun beating on your back,
The heart and mind disconnect—
Your weary legs, your sleepless mind...
Standing there, on the front line.
One kill, and then another
.........a child of a mother
Day in and day out
Returning home with great doubt......
You did your job.
Completed your mission.
A good soldier you were.
A good soldier you were.....
Forgive yourself, Forgive today
Allow the piece of you that died that day,
to drift, drift away.

A soldier no more,
Returning as a husband, father,
brother or son.
A soldier you were.
A soldier no more---
A man who forgives himself
for the duty he performed....
A man returns from battle
and stands before all, to be adorned.

JEAN VAN KINGSLEY

If your partner has PTSD, chances are that you are his caregiver. That means you face all the stress that comes from caring for a loved one with a chronic problem: dealing with his symptoms, financial strain, loss of friends, the burden it creates for the children, and even loss of intimacy. But the stress does not have to get to you. Your partner is your journey partner, your sidekick. You can learn how to deal with his PTSD so that you don't lose him- or yourself—along the way.

When Your Partner Is a Veteran with PTSD

Any war, regardless of its origin, purpose, and time, results in death and destruction. The terrors of war could haunt its survivors, especially the heroic survivors—the veterans—in flashbacks and nightmares, even during daily activities. These

What Nurses Know...

The rate of PTSD is three times higher among deployed military men and women exposed to combat compared to military members who were not deployed.

terrors can create unseen wounds that go untreated, affecting both the veterans and their families. Partners of veterans with PTSD have reported lower overall satisfaction, more caregiver burden, and poorer psychological adjustment than do partners of veterans without PTSD. Moreover, they were also highly distressed. Fortunately, the veterans' posttraumatic stress, as it has become known in recent years, has been well studied, providing an escape for those who suffered and their families.

The Effects of War

War is epic trauma. During wartime, military personnel are likely to be exposed to a number of traumatic or highly stressful events. Yet they do not all develop PTSD. As you read in Chapter 2, some people may be more vulnerable to developing PTSD than others. Remember the "perfect storm" where PTSD is most likely a combination of four things? It also applies to your partner and includes his genetics, particularly predisposition

PTSD Care for Veterans, Military, and Families
- *Military OneSource exists to help Active-Duty, Guard, and Reserve service members and their families with just about any need: education, relocation, parenting, stress, and more. Call 24/7 for counseling and many resources: 1-800-342-9647.*
- *All VA Medical Centers provide PTSD care, as do many VA clinics.*
- *Your partner can call the 24/7 Veteran Combat Call Center at 1-877-927-8387 (WAR-VETS) to talk to another combat Veteran.*
- *To contact the Department of Defense Outreach Center for Psychological Health and Traumatic Brain Injury, call 1-866-966-1020 or email resources@dcoeoutreach.org*

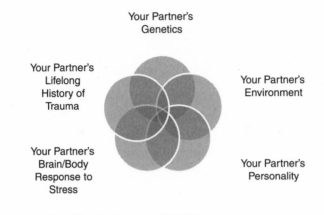

Your Partner's
Genetics

Your Partner's
Lifelong
History of
Trauma

Your Partner's
Environment

Your Partner's
Brain/Body
Response to
Stress

Your Partner's
Personality

Figure 9.1 Combined Causes of PTSD

to anxiety and depression; his life experience, including traumas since childhood; his personality; his brain/body response
to stress; and his environment.

There are several general risk factors that may have made
your partner more prone to PTSD. These include: experiencing
intense or long-lasting trauma; going through other trauma
earlier in life; having mental health problems such as anxiety
or depression, or having relatives with mental health problems;
not having a good family and friend support system; and having
been neglected or abused as a child. Military deployment adds
even more risk factors. Those who felt they were in great danger
of death, were shot or seriously injured, saw someone wounded
or killed, or had exposure to violence before recruit training are
more at risk for developing PTSD.

Military personnel are taught to be ready for war. They have
to face catastrophe, remain on high alert, engage in killing, and
sometimes see atrocities that may be distanced in the civilian
world. When they return, they come home with the haunted imagery of death and mutilation of their comrades, the guilt of being
the survivor, and the constant morality and identity struggle of
being a life-saver versus life-taker. Anger and other symptoms
of posttraumatic stress can translate to years of drug addiction,

VA National Caregiver Support Line:
1-855-260-3274

substance abuse, and/or violence. During these times, military personnel can also be distanced from their family and society, have the strong desire to be alone, and say and do hurtful things before they find the help they need.

Your Partner's PTSD Symptoms

The symptoms of PTSD are fully discussed in Chapter 3. However, here is a quick review. There are four types of PTSD symptoms:

- *Re-experiencing symptoms (also called reliving the event)*: Trauma memories can pop up at any time, and your partner may feel the same fear and horror he did when the event took place. He may have nightmares or flashbacks. These symptoms may be set off by a trigger, such as hearing a car backfire, which can bring back memories of gunfire and war for a combat veteran.
- *Avoiding situations that remind him of the event*: He may try to avoid situations or people that trigger memories of the trauma, and he may avoid talking about it. For example, he may refuse to watch movies about war. He may also bury himself in his work to avoid even thinking about the trauma.
- *Feeling numb:* Your partner may have difficulty expressing his feelings, or he may have trouble just having feelings. This may make him distance himself from you to the point where he does not want emotional or physical contact, even sexual relations. This is another way to avoid memories; it is not a direct reflection on you. He may lose interest in previously enjoyed activities altogether.

- *Hyperarousal (feeling keyed up)*: Your partner may be jittery or always on the lookout for danger. This can result in his having trouble sleeping and concentrating, fearing for his safety, and being easily startled. It can also cause him to suddenly become angry or irritable. This anger can cause major disruption in your relationship and will be covered in more detail in the following section.

The symptoms of PTSD can be frightening. They can disrupt your partner's life and make it hard for him to continue with his daily activities. He may also have some of the collateral damage discussed in Chapter 4, including alcohol or drug problems; feelings of hopelessness, shame, or despair; employment problems; and physical symptoms. Without intervention, your partner's PTSD can result in relationship problems including divorce and violence.

When Your Partner Gets Angry

Everyone experiences anger. Anger is part of life, just like joy, sadness, and jealousy. It's a normal, usually healthy, human emotion. Anger is an adaptive response to threats, and it inspires powerful feelings that allow us to defend ourselves and fight when attacked. We need a certain amount of anger to survive. But when anger gets out of control and turns to destruction, it leads to problems with relationships, problems at work, and problems in your partner's overall quality of life.

Anger is an emotional state that varies in intensity from slight irritability to full blown rage. It raises your heart rate and blood pressure and causes the release of stress hormones. Anger has three components:

1. The first component is the emotion itself, a feeling experienced when a need is frustrated or a goal is blocked. The

feeling can be brought on by several things, such as conflict over possessions, physical assault, verbal conflict, rejection, and a desire to not comply with another's wishes.

2. The second component is the expression of anger, which varies from person to person. Your partner uses a variety of conscious and unconscious processes to deal with anger, and he may use one or more of the four main approaches to dealing with it: expressing, diverting, suppressing, or exploding.

- Expressing anger in an assertive, nonaggressive manner is the most appropriate way to deal with anger. To do this your partner needs to learn how to make his needs clear and how to get them met without hurting others. Being assertive means being respectful to himself and others.

- Diverting anger allows your partner to stop and redirect his feelings toward something constructive, like sports.

- When anger is suppressed, your partner disallows himself an outward expression of his anger. He may grimace, sulk, or talk but do little to solve the problem or confrontation, or he may try to escape from or evade the issue. He may then turn the anger inward, on himself. This can cause depression. Suppressed anger can create other problems such as passive-aggressive behavior (getting back at people indirectly), or a personality that is cynical and hostile. People who constantly put down others and criticize everything around them have not learned to deal with anger effectively.

- Exploding measures are aggressive. He may express anger with revenge by physically or verbally retaliating against others.

3. The third component is the understanding and evaluation of anger. Your partner must learn to understand his anger in order to regulate it. However, his ability to reflect on his anger may be limited. Therefore, he needs your support.

SOME PEOPLE ARE MORE ANGRY THAN OTHERS

Some people are hotheads. They get angry more easily and more quickly than other people. Easily angered people have a low tolerance for frustration, inconvenience, and annoyance. They don't take things in stride, and get particularly annoyed over little things.

How do people get this way? For one thing, there may be genetic causes. People are born with unique temperaments, and some are simply irritable and easily angered from day one. Family background may play a role in becoming easily angered as many hotheads come from families that are chaotic and disruptive. Finally, society regards anger as negative. Therefore, these people don't learn how to handle it constructively.

CONTROLLING ANGER

We live in a tumultuous world where we see violence on a daily basis through the media. This may create a powerful influence on how your partner views the world and how he solves problems, especially if he already feels in constant danger from his PTSD. However, he must learn to recognize his own angry feelings, express anger nonviolently, communicate anger in a positive way, calm himself, problem solve, remove himself from an angry situation, and avoid becoming a victim of someone else's anger. Try the following:

1. *Help him to know when he's angry.* People feel anger in different ways. Some breathe faster, some feel their muscles

What Nurses Know...

The media can affect how we think and feel. Minimize household use of violent programming and electronic gaming.

and fists clench, some feel their face turn red. Others want to scream or break something. Work with your partner to find out how he feels anger.

2. Teach him to gain control. He should admit to himself that he's angry and try to figure out why. Have him say, "I feel angry when (something happens) because (what it does)." This helps him realize that there are always hidden feelings and actions behind angry emotions.

3. Have him ask himself if the situation is important enough to get angry about. Sometimes his anger may not really be directed at the immediate situation. It may relate back to the trauma.

4. Demonstrate how to deal with anger:

   • Communicate. Angry people jump to conclusions, many of which can be inaccurate. Tell him to slow down and think, and not say the first thing that comes to his mind. He should think carefully about what he wants to say, and he should listen to what the other person is saying. Encourage him to express his feelings in a variety of ways. He can talk it over with you, a friend, or his therapist.

   • Problem solve. Your partner can't escape problems that cause anger and frustration. He needs to use his problem solving skills, and he needs to accept that some problems are not solvable. When faced with an unsolvable problem, help your partner focus on coping and accepting the situation for what it is.

   • Change the environment. The easiest way to avoid conflict is to simply walk away from the problem and cool off. Encourage him to remove himself from the situation if he feels that he's losing control. Sometimes it may be necessary for you to intervene and restructure the environment for him. You may also need to change your actual living environment. Chaos leads to frustration and confusion, while a clean, orderly environment helps to create a peaceful atmosphere.

   • Use humor. Humor acts as the perfect antidote for anger in many situations. It helps to balance perspectives, and it often defuses the situation. You don't want your partner to laugh off his problems; you want him to use humor to face them more constructively. Use silly humor, not sarcastic humor. Sarcasm is simply another form of anger.

- Encourage him to change the way he thinks. When your partner gets angry, he thinks in very overdramatic and exaggerated terms. Help him replace theses thoughts with more rational ones. For example, instead of his thinking that "everything is destroyed," encourage his to think that "it's not the end of the world." Persuade him to not use words such as "always" and "never." These words tend to make your partner feel justified about his anger, and that there's no way to solve the problems.

5. Give his a "honey-do and don't" list for dealing with anger:
   Do:
   - Count to ten.
   - Talk to someone about the situation.
   - Write about it in a journal.
   - Paint a picture of his anger or the situation.
   - Give someone a hug.
   - Play with the kids or the dog.
   - Do something active, like exercise.
   - Sing or listen to music.
   - Pound a peg board or play the drums.
   - Punch a punching bag.
   - Think happy thoughts.
   - Tell a joke.
   - Watch a funny movie.
   - Walk away from the problem.
   - Play ball.
   - Ask someone for help.
   Don't:
   - Hurt yourself.
   - Hurt someone else.
   - Hurt an animal.

- Destroy property.
- Scream at people.
- Have a tantrum.

Chronic anger always results in some form of destruction, whether to others or your partner. It gets in the way of daily living and ruins relationships. If your partner experiences chronic anger, seek the guidance and support of a counselor or family therapist.

CONFLICT RESOLUTION

Anger and PTSD create conflict. Everyone, including your partner, is an individual with separate needs, experiences, and ways of viewing the world. Thus conflict is inevitable. It's a normal part of close relationships, and typically, the closer the relationship, the greater the opportunities for conflict. Conflict itself isn't necessarily dangerous; it may even indicate growth. However, if not handled properly, conflict can eventually damage and even destroy relationships.

Conflict usually accompanies anger, so anger management plays a role in conflict resolution. When your partner attempts to deal with conflict through anger, he runs the risk of creating distrust and distance. If he acts without thinking things through, he can cause the conflict to escalate. If he represses the anger, it can turn into hostility and resentment.

Conflict resolution involves negotiation, mediation, or consensual decision making. Assist your partner in settling conflicts by teaching him the following strategies.

1. Define the problem and separate yourself from it. All problems contain both substantive and relationship issues. Separating these two issues allows both sides to work as a team, side-by-side, to attack the problem instead of each other. Your partner may need to think through his feelings to discover what's really bothering him.

2. Decide what each person wants. Only one person should speak at a time. When one speaks, the other listens. Your partner should ask the other person to express his or her own interests and not assume he knows what the other person is thinking.

3. Talk about the issue at hand, don't get distracted by other issues, and don't bring up things from the past.

4. Concentrate on the interests, not the positions. Positions are the things people want; interests are why they want them. Compromising on positions tends to result only in temporary agreements because the real interests haven't been addressed.

5. Look for alternatives that let both parties get what they want. Brainstorm to formulate a wide range of options. During brainstorming, postpone criticism and evaluation of the ideas being generated. Instead, think about the problem in different ways to build on the idea already presented.

6. Negotiate. Work out agreements for change. Compromise on who does what.

7. Firm up the agreement. Verbally go over the plan, or write it down if necessary. Ensure that both parties understand and agree to it.

8. Review and renegotiate when needed. Come up with a timeframe to try out a new plan.

Your partner must feel safe in voicing disagreements with you. He needs to trust that the discussion won't get out of control, and that you won't abandon him or take advantage of him. This provides the baseline for him to resolve conflicts with others. When conflicts are resolved constructively, both sides win.

Common Problems of Partners of Veterans with PTSD

Your partner's PTSD can affect your relationship, your mental health, and your family. Compared to veterans without PTSD, veterans with PTSD have more marital troubles. They share less of their thoughts and feelings, and they have intimacy problems as sexual problems tend to be higher in combat veterans with PTSD. The National Vietnam Veterans Readjustment Study (NVVRS) compared veterans with PTSD to those without PTSD and found that Vietnam veterans with PTSD got divorced twice as much, were three times more likely to divorce two or more times, and tended to have shorter relationships. Other issues that came up in the comparison study:

- Family violence: Families of veterans with PTSD experience more physical and verbal aggression, and more instances of family violence.
- Mental health of partners: PTSD can affect the mental health and life satisfaction of a veteran's partner. Partners of Vietnam veterans with PTSD reported lower levels of happiness; less satisfaction in their lives; more demoralization (discouragement); and about half have felt "on the verge of a nervous breakdown."

Partners have a difficult time coping with their partner's PTSD symptoms. They feel stressed because their own needs are not being met. Partners may exhibit secondary traumatization, the indirect impact of trauma on those close to the survivor. Partners also experience caregiver burden. Wives of PTSD-diagnosed Veterans tend to take on a bigger share of household tasks, and do more care of children and the extended family. They also feel that they must take care of the veteran and attend closely to the veteran's problems. Partners are well aware of what can trigger symptoms of PTSD, and they work hard to lessen the effects of those triggers. Caregiver burden includes practical problems such as strain on the family finances and emotional strain of caring for someone who is ill. The worse the veteran's PTSD symptoms, the more severe is the caregiver burden.

HELP FOR PARTNERS OF VETERANS WITH PTSD

The first step for partners of veterans with PTSD is to obtain information to better understand PTSD and its impact on families. Some effective strategies for treatment include:

- Education for the whole family about the effects of trauma on survivors and their families
- Support groups for both partners and veterans
- Individual therapy for both partners and veterans, as well as the children, if needed
- Couples or family counseling

PTSD programs and veterans centers have begun to offer group, couples, and individual counseling for family members of veterans. The message for partners is that problems are common when living with a traumatized veteran, and treatment may be useful to partners as they search for better family relationships and mental health.

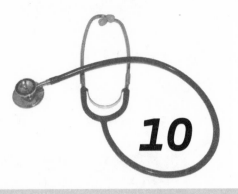

Kids Stuff: When Your Child Has PTSD

"Nervous, distracted, unable to concentrate. We thought he had ADHD. None of us connected the car accident to his problems. Who would have thought my five year old would get PTSD?" TAWANDA

Adults are not the only ones who can get PTSD. The disorder can affect children as young as 3 years old. The occurrence of PTSD in children varies according to several factors, including the type of trauma, how close the child was to the trauma, and the reaction of the child's parents. For example, after witnessing the death of a parent or witnessing domestic violence, the rate can be as high as 95% to 100%, while the rate for witnessing a school shooting is 40%. As you can see, the prevalence of PTSD is considerable among high-risk children who have experienced specific traumatic events, such as abuse or disasters. Your child

What Nurses Know...

Severe emotional trauma can have a huge effect on children. Trauma can undercut a child's sense of security causing the child to believe that their parents cannot protect them from harm.

may live in a safe home, but PTSD can also result from severe accidents, floods, severe burns, or the suicide of a friend.

PTSD: Kids Are Not Just Small Adults

Childhood trauma can take many forms, including physical or sexual abuse, disasters, and traumatic death of a loved one, as well as emotional abuse or neglect. However, severe trauma can have significant effects on a child's development. Trauma can undermine a child's sense of security, as well as cause the child to believe that the parents cannot protect the child from harm. Premature destruction of these beliefs can have intense negative consequences on your child's development. Traumatized youth are frequently preoccupied with danger and vulnerability, which can sometimes lead to misperceptions of danger, even in situations that are not threatening. Once posttraumatic stress

What Nurses Know...

A recent survey confirms that most of the children in the United States are exposed to violence on a daily basis, and more than 60% of the children surveyed were exposed to violence within the past year.

symptoms emerge, PTSD leads to changes that impact brain function in developing children and adolescents.

Unfortunately, children can be exposed to a multitude of traumas during their lifetimes:

- *Community violence* includes violence in which the persons involved are not family members. This violence may include brutal acts such as shootings, rapes, stabbings, and beatings, and children may experience trauma as victims, witnesses, or perpetrators. School violence includes student or teacher victimization, threats to or injury of students, fights at school, and students carrying weapons. It may be possible that children can develop PTSD from severe bullying.
- *Child neglect* occurs when a parent or caregiver does not give a child the care he or she needs, even though that adult can afford to give that care or is offered help to give that care. Neglect can mean not giving food, clothing, and shelter, as well as not providing a child with medical or mental health treatment, not giving prescribed medicines the child needs, neglecting the child's education, and exposing a child to dangerous environments. It can also mean poor supervision for a child, abandoning a child, or expelling the child from home.
- *Physical abuse* means causing or attempting to cause physical pain or injury by punching, beating, kicking, burning, or harming a child in other ways. Injury can also occur when a punishment is not appropriate for a child's age or condition.
- *Sexual abuse* includes a wide range of sexual behaviors between a child and adult or sometimes between a child and another child/adolescent. Behaviors often involve bodily contact, such as sexual kissing, touching, fondling of genitals, and intercourse. However, behaviors may not involve contact, such as of genital exposure ("flashing"), verbal pressure for sex, sexual talk over the Internet, and sexual exploitation for purposes of prostitution or pornography.

- *Complex trauma* describes children's exposure to multiple or prolonged traumatic events and the impact of this exposure on their development. It usually involves the simultaneous or sequential occurrence of child abuse and domestic violence that is chronic, begins in early childhood, and occurs within the child's family system. The exposure to these initial trauma experiences, and their resulting emotional turmoil and loss of the ability to respond to danger cues, usually sets off a chain of events that leads to later trauma exposure in adolescence and adulthood. Thus, young children who are exposed to child abuse and domestic violence may continue to experience more trauma as teens and adults because they do not know what do to when they are in danger.

- *Domestic violence,* also called intimate partner violence or battering, includes actual or threatened physical, sexual, or emotional abuse between two adults who are involved in an intimate relationship, such as a husband and wife. Domestic violence can happen in a current or former spouse or partner relationship, and it can happen in either a heterosexual or same-sex relationship.

- *Early childhood trauma* typically refers to the traumatic experiences that occur to children aged 0 to 6 years of age that can be the result of intentional violence or the result of natural disaster, accidents, or war. Young children also may experience traumatic stress in response to the sudden loss of a parent or caregiver.

- *Medical trauma* refers to reactions that children and their families may have to pain, injury, and serious illness, or to invasive procedures (such as surgery) or treatments (such as burn care) that are sometimes frightening. Children and their families may become anxious, irritable, or on edge, and may have unwanted thoughts or nightmares about the experience. This may cause some to avoid going to the doctor or the hospital or to lose interest in being with friends and family and things they used to enjoy. The children may not do well at school, work, or at home.

- *Disasters* can be natural (tornadoes, hurricanes, fires, floods, and earthquakes) or man-made (terrorism or nuclear reactor explosion). Terrorism includes attacks by individuals acting in isolation (for example, sniper attacks), as well as attacks by groups or people acting for groups (the September 11, 2001 attacks on the United States). Disasters can leave children feeling confused, frightened, and insecure.

- *Traumatic grief* may occur following the death of someone important to the child, if the child views the loss as traumatic. The death may have been sudden and unexpected or anticipated. The distinguishing feature of childhood traumatic grief is that trauma symptoms interfere with the child's ability to go through the typical process of bereavement. The child experiences symptoms so severe that any thoughts or reminders—even happy ones—about the deceased can lead to frightening thoughts, images, and/or memories of how the person died.

If your child has PTSD, she may experience many of the same symptoms as adults. However these symptoms may look different because children have greater difficulty telling their thoughts and feelings. They also have some differences with

What Nurses Know...

Children who are the victims of severe animal attacks should be considered at risk for PTSD.

To Help Your Children Deal with Trauma
- *Reassure them that you will do your best to keep them and their loved ones safe.*
- *Tell them the event was not their fault.*
- *Remind them that you love them, that you support them, and that you will be with them whenever possible.*
- *Encourage them to talk and ask questions.*
- *Listen to them.*
- *Let them talk, write, or draw about their feelings.*
- *Answer questions honestly.*
- *Limit excessive TV watching and listening to graphic replays of the traumatic event.*
- *Stick to daily routines as much as possible.*
- *Allow children to be sad and to cry.*

their re-experiencing symptoms. Thus, if your child is young, she may:

- Display repetitive play that reenacts some of the trauma, such as repeatedly submerging her doll if your family experienced flooding;
- Have frightening dreams without recognizable content (wake up sweating and crying, but can't remember the dream); or
- Act out the trauma as if it were recurring (falling to the ground when she hears noise that sounds like gunfire).

PTSD can have a considerably negative impact on your child's life. Besides the usual PTSD symptoms, your child can suffer from a decreased ability to participate in normal school and social activities.

PTSD symptoms vary greatly among children and adolescents depending upon the traumatic event itself, its severity, its duration, and the child's developmental age at the time of the

What Nurses Know...

PTSD in children may mimic other childhood mental health disorders. These include: acute stress disorder, adjustment disorder, attention deficit hyperactivity disorder (ADHD) and other disruptive disorders, depression, and other anxiety disorders and sleep disorders. Symptoms may overlap, and some children may suffer from more than one mental health disorder.

trauma. Even children who do display the classic symptoms of PTSD may do so differently than adults. The way a child re-experiences and shows his feelings of distress related to a traumatic event is also likely to change as the child ages.

- *Young children (under age 5)* may reenact their trauma through play and drawings. Their play themes may relate directly to the trauma or they may play in a symbolic manner. Thus one child who was victimized by violence may act out the violence on her doll or stuffed animals, while another who was victimized by the same type of trauma may play-act that he is killing a monster. Whatever the type of re-enacted play, the child may repeat it over and over.
- *School-age children (ages 5 to 12)* may not have flashbacks or problems remembering parts of the trauma the way adults do. However, they might place the traumatic events in the wrong order, and think that there were signs that the trauma was going to happen. Thus, they think that they will be able to see this sign before another traumatic event happens, believing that if they pay attention, they can avoid future traumas. Some school-age children may act out the trauma in their

play; others may fit it into their daily lives by doing things such as carrying a gun to class.

- *Adolescents (13 to 18)* may show the same signs as adults, which include invasive thoughts (that they may not talk about), restlessness, aggression, difficulty sleeping, and difficulty concentrating. They may also experience loss of interest in previously enjoyed activities, withdrawal from family and peers, and changes in their attitudes. The onset of PTSD during adolescence can have a damaging impact since it may impair the development of life skills needed for independence and self-sufficiency. Mastery of these skills occurs within a limited time and must be developed in order for the adolescent to meet the demands of the adult world. If these skills are not achieved before the onset of adulthood, the impairment can last throughout life. Teens who suffer with chronic PTSD triggered by repeated or prolonged trauma may suffer primarily from numbing, sadness, restricted affect, detachment, self-injury, substance abuse, and aggressive outbursts.

Children and adolescents may also demonstrate impulsivity and inattentiveness, which negatively affects their academic achievement. They may isolate themselves from others and withdraw from their peers, and they may demonstrate "backward" behaviors such as bedwetting, soiling, and thumb-sucking.

What Nurses Know ...

Children with PTSD may be more attracted to joining gangs. Gangs act as families to some children, but they also can offer a sense of safety and control, and provide rules that are often missing in the lives of traumatized youth. They also provide an outlet for negative feelings.

Possible Associated Problems

As with adults, PTSD can have co-occurring problems, and these can be considerable in children: mood disorders, conduct disorders, substance abuse, risk-taking that poses considerable danger, eating disorders, sexual acting out, depression, the full range of anxiety disorders, violence, and difficulty concentrating.

MOOD DISORDERS

The most common mood disorders found in children and adolescents are major depressive disorder, reactive depression, dysthymic disorder, and bipolar disorder. Mood disorders such as depression increase the risk for suicide, which reaches its peak during the adolescent years.

Major Depressive Disorder

Major depression is a serious condition that is characterized by one or more major depressive episodes. Children become sad and lose interest in the activities that please them most. They criticize themselves and believe that others criticize them. They feel pessimistic, helpless, and unloved. They experience difficulty making decisions, have trouble concentrating, and may neglect their appearance and hygiene. Feelings of hopelessness can arise and evolve into thoughts or actions of suicide.

Depressed children and teens often act irritable and sometimes become aggressive. Some teens feel a surge of energy, occupying every minute of their day with activity to avoid their depression. Depressed youths may become anxious and have separation fears, and they may have physical complaints, like headaches, stomach aches and other aches and pains.

Reactive Depression

This is the most common form of depression in children and teens. This depression is usually short-lived and results as a response to an adverse experience, such as rejection, a slight, a letdown, or a loss. Thus, children can develop reactive depression to divorce, moving, a death, or changing schools.

Dysthymic Disorder

Dysthymia is similar to major depression with fewer symptoms and a more chronic course. Because of its persistent nature, dysthymia tends to interfere with normal development. The child feels depressed for most of the day, on most days, and for several years, with an average duration of four years. Some are depressed for so long that they don't recognize that their state as abnormal and thus don't complain of being depressed.

Symptoms of dysthymia include low energy or fatigue, changes in eating and/or sleeping patterns (too much or too little of either), poor concentration, and hopelessness. About 70% of dysthymic children eventually experience an episode of major depression.

Bipolar Disorder

Also called manic-depressive disorder, bipolar disorder typically includes episodes of depression and mania. Mania is characterized by an extremely elevated energy level, irritability, fast speech, racing thoughts, decreased sleep, and impulsive behaviors. When manic, children are overconfident, and they talk rapidly, loudly, and a lot. They can't sleep, rarely eat, feel like their thoughts are racing, and do things quickly in a creative but chaotic, disorganized manner. Some may experience delusions of great self-importance and engage in risky behavior, such as careless sex or fast driving.

Suicide

Although somewhat unusual in younger children, suicide is not uncommon in teenagers. As a matter of fact, it's the third leading cause of death in people ages 15 to 24, and rates for younger teens are rising. Females attempt suicide more often than males, but males are more successful in actually committing suicide because they use more lethal weapons.

Most victims of suicide have a psychiatric illness, particularly major depression or bipolar disorder. Other victims frequently had severe anxiety, exhibited violent and impulsive behavior, had no plans for the future, or were deficient in social skills. Most attempted suicides and completed suicides are preceded by a precipitant, such as a relationship break-up, family or school violence, rejection, sexual abuse, pregnancy, or a sexually transmitted disease. Drugs and alcohol play a key role in suicide, as do exposure to suicide in family or friends and availability of weapons. "Copycat" suicides remain common among teenagers, especially vulnerable ones.

Your child is at increased risk for suicide if he fits any of the following risk factors. If any of these apply to your child, talk to your child's healthcare provider:
- *Previous suicide attempts (risk is greater if attempts happened in past 3 months)*
- *Psychiatric disorder*
- *Family member with mood disorder, past suicide attempt, or successful suicide*
- *Child or family member with substance abuse problem*
- *Family discord*
- *Impulsiveness*
- *Hostility*
- *Poor social skills*
- *School problems, including truancy*
- *Romantic break-up*
- *Homosexual or bisexual preference*

Bring your child to an emergency facility immediately for any of these:
- *Stating he or she wants to hurt or kill him-/herself*

- *Any suicide plan*
- *Irrational speech*
- *Sudden alienation from family*
- *Sudden interest or loss of interest in religion*
- *Taking unnecessary risks*
- *Hears voices or sees visions*
- *Drug and alcohol abuse*
- *Giving away possessions*
- *Writing notes or poems about death*
- *Preoccupation with death-themed music, movies, art, or video games*
- *Feelings of hopelessness*
- *Statements like, "You won't have to worry about me anymore."*

CONDUCT DISORDER

Conduct disorder is a repetitive and persistent pattern of behavior in which the child violates the basic rights of others or the major rules and values of society. Behaviors include aggression toward people and animals; starting physical fights; carrying a weapon that can cause serious physical harm to others; destruction of property; deceitfulness; theft; and serious violations of rules. Conduct disorder can have a childhood, adolescence, or unspecified onset, and can range in severity from mild to severe.

What Nurses Know...

Children with conduct disorder are at risk for developing PTSD because of their risk-taking behaviors.

Attention Deficit Hyperactivity Disorder

The main symptoms of attention deficit hyperactivity disorder (ADHD) are inattention, hyperactivity, and impulsivity. Most children experience fleeting episodes of these behaviors, especially younger ones. The symptoms indicate ADHD when they occur over an extended period of time, appear in different settings, and occur at a level that impairs the child's performance. Children affected by ADHD may engage in a wide range of problem behaviors that frustrate and disrupt family, school, and peer relationships. Their inability to pay attention and sit still in class may lead to school failure, truancy, and dropping out. Untreated, ADHD can continue into adolescence and adulthood. These children may also have co-occurring conduct disorders, and may abuse substances and engage in antisocial behavior.

Other Anxiety Disorders

Anxiety disorders are the most common psychiatric conditions found in adolescents, and the majority of adult anxiety disorders begin in childhood, adolescence, and early adulthood. Children with anxiety disorders are usually so afraid, worried, or uneasy that they cannot function normally. PTSD is an anxiety disorder, but your child may also suffer from a co-existing anxiety disorder.

- Children with *general anxiety disorder* have excessive worry, anxiety, and apprehension occurring on most days. Children with general anxiety disorder worry about anything and everything. They get restless and easily fatigued. They have trouble concentrating or feel like their mind goes blank.
- Children with *separation anxiety disorder* experience intense anxiety, sometimes to the point of panic, when separated from a parent or other loved one. The anxiety is so severe that the child cannot perform daily activities, and becomes preoccupied with gloomy fears of harm or fears that the parents will not return. Separation anxiety can grow into school phobia,

whereby the child will refuse to go to school because of fear of separation from the parents.

- Children can get *obsessive-compulsive disorder (OCD)*. Once thought to only occur in adults (think Melvin Udall in the movie *As Good as It Gets* or TV character Adrian Monk), this disorder is now more frequently diagnosed in children. Children with OCD have persistent obsessions (intrusive, unwanted thoughts, images, or urges) and compulsions (intensive, uncontrollable, and repetitive behaviors or mental acts related to the obsessions). These obsessions and compulsions cause distress and consume a huge amount of the child's time. The most common obsessions involve dirtiness and contamination, repeated doubts, and the need to have things a specific way. Frequent compulsions include repetitive hand washing, using tissues or gloved hands to touch things, touching and counting things, checking locks, counting rituals, repeating actions, and requesting reassurance.
- Children may have a *specific phobia*, which is an excessive, persistent, unreasonable fear of a specific object or event, such as snakes, spiders, computers, close spaces, heights, flying, and getting injured. Exposure to the object or situation immediately provokes anxiety. The distress is so severe that it interferes with the child's functioning or routine.
- Children may also have *social phobia*. These children have a serious fear of one social situations in which they are exposed to unfamiliar people or scrutiny by others. Exposure to these situations causes significant anxiety and possible panic despite knowing that the fear is unreasonable. This fear can cause children to avoid such situations, leading to marked interference in life.
- Like adults, children can suffer from *panic disorder* and have panic attacks. The attacks are sudden episodes of intense fear that are usually accompanied by a feeling of doom or impending danger. And like adults, they have many of the same panic symptoms: palpitations, sweating, shortness of breath or

What Nurses Know ...

Four words you need to know: Your child can heal.

feeling smothered, trembling or shaking, nausea and abdominal pain, dizziness, lightheadedness, feeling faint, sense of unreality or being detached from one's self, fear of losing control or going crazy, numbness and tingling, and chills or hot flashes.

Treatment of Children and Adolescents with PTSD

For some children, the symptoms of PTSD go away on their own after a few months; for others, the symptoms last for years without treatment. Because PTSD symptoms can greatly disrupt your child's development and because some children with PTSD also have other disorders, your child should be evaluated by an appropriate mental healthcare professional. If you think your child may have PTSD, talk to your child's healthcare provider.

As with adults, there are multiple treatment options for children with PTSD. These include psychotherapies, medications, and alternative treatments. Your child may do best with one or a combination of treatments.

Treatment should focus on the multiple emotional and behavioral problems that can arise, such as depression, anxiety, impulsive behavior, substance abuse, aggression, eating disorders, sexual acting out, labile mood, rage, panic attacks, and detaching. Treatment of these problems may involve medication, psychotherapy, or a combination of these, as well as supportive treatments. Specific treatment depends on your child's development and symptoms, as well as the nature of the trauma.

The first step is helping your child gain a sense of mastery over the trauma and helping the child feel safe again. For older children, gaining a sense of mastery includes the ability to recall and talk about the trauma without detaching or feeling over-whelmed. Meditation and relaxation training may help the child to do this. Play helps younger children work through the trauma, but the play often breaks down in PTSD, and may turn into repet-itive reenactment that is not enjoyable and that requires other interventions to allow the child to feel safe again.

It is important that you and your child not view your child's symptoms as shameful. You need to understand that the repeated recollections, numbing, and hyperarousal are natural responses to trauma and not signs of serious mental illness or weakness. You should also avoid burdening your child with any of your own incorrect feelings that your child is permanently damaged.

PSYCHOTHERAPY

There are three different types of psychotherapy for PTSD: cri-sis management, cognitive-behavior therapy, and eye movement desensitization and reprocessing (EMDR).

Psychological First Aid/Crisis Management

Psychological first aid helps survivors in the immediate after-math of a traumatic event. It can help everyone from children to adults to families. This therapy reduces the initial distress caused by the event and acknowledges the seriousness of the experience of danger and the increased feelings of vulnerabil-ity that often follow. Psychological first aid fosters long- and short-term adaptability, basic functioning, and coping skills. It can be used in schools and traditional settings. It involves pro-viding comfort and support by letting children know that their reactions are normal, and teaches calming and problem-solving skills. Psychological first aid also helps caregivers deal with changes in the child's feelings and behavior. While beneficial for many children, those with more severe symptoms may be referred for added treatment.

Cognitive-Behavioral Therapy

Cognitive–behavioral therapy techniques have been shown to be effective in treating children and adolescents with PTSD. Cognitive–behavioral therapy can reduce serious trauma reactions, other anxiety and depressive symptoms, and behavioral problems. One type is called trauma-focused cognitive-behavioral therapy, during which the child may talk about his or her memory of the trauma. Trauma-focused cognitive-behavioral therapy also includes techniques that help lower worry and stress and help teach the child how to assert him- or herself. The therapy may involve learning to change incorrect thoughts or beliefs about the trauma, such as the world is not a safe place. The child can be taught to remember scary memories at his or her own pace and to relax while they are thinking about the trauma. That way, they learn that they do not have to be afraid of their memories. Cognitive-behavioral therapy often uses training for parents and caregivers as well, and it is important for caregivers to understand the effects of PTSD and to learn coping skills that will help them help their children.

Eye Movement Desensitization and Reprocessing (EMDR)

Eye movement desensitization and reprocessing (EMDR) is a newer form of cognitive behavioral therapy. Your child concentrates on the most distressing part of a traumatic memory while moving her eyes rapidly from side to side (following the therapist's fingers). After the initial focus on the memory, your child is asked to report anything that "came up," whether an image, thought, emotion, or physical sensation (all are common). The focus of the next set is determined by your child's status.

Play Therapy

Play therapy can help young children with PTSD who are not able to deal with the trauma more directly. Play therapists uses games, drawings, and other methods to help children process their traumatic memories.

MEDICATION

Selective serotonin reuptake inhibitors (SSRIs) are the medications of choice for managing anxiety, depression, avoidance behavior, and intrusive recollections. Two SSRIs used for children are Zoloft (sertraline) and Prozac (fluoxetine). Inderal (propranolol) and Tenex (guanfacine) may be useful for the treatment of hyperarousal and re-experiencing symptoms. Mood stabilizers, such as Tegretol (carbamazepine), can help deal with increased arousal and impulsivity. Antipsychotics are only used for children who do not respond to other medications or when marked agitation or psychosis is present.

Stress: The Good, The Bad, and Dealing With It All

Stress overload can cause your child to be withdrawn, depressed, and suicidal, and it can give him a number of physical ailments.

What Nurses Know...

It is important to choose the right therapist for your child. Use the tips in Chapter 7, but make sure that you choose a therapist who is experienced in working with children and adolescents. Schedule a consultation appointment to see if you and your child are comfortable with the therapist.

What Nurses Know . . .

Some children withstand an onslaught of stressors. No matter what happens, they bounce back in the face of stressful events and situations. These children tend to have specific characteristics:

- *They have a loving relationship with at least one adult, and connections with adults outside the family.*
- *They believe in their own effectiveness, and that they are lovable and worthwhile.*
- *They can solve problems effectively.*
- *They believe that they have the ability to make things better for themselves.*
- *They have spiritual resources.*

It can also make the child irritable, disobedient, and uncooperative. He can become aggressive and get into fights, and stress overload can propel him into drugs, alcohol, and delinquent behaviors such as truancy, stealing, and fire setting.

Chronic stress leads to feelings of being "stressed out" or "burned out." Stress may not be easy to recognize because it often affects the body, leading you to believe that your child is ill rather than stressed. Signs of chronic stress include:

- Headaches, backaches, chest pain, stomachaches, indigestion, nausea, or diarrhea
- Rashes
- Overeating or undereating
- Sleep disturbances (too much sleep, restless sleep, difficulty falling asleep, difficulty staying asleep, waking up early)
- Twitching
- Having trouble concentrating or with school work

- Feeling anxious or worried
- Feeling inadequate, frustrated, helpless, or overwhelmed
- Feeling bored or dissatisfied
- Feeling pressured, tense, irritable, angry, or hostile
- Aggressive behavior
- Substance abuse
- Excessive or inappropriate crying
- Avoiding others

CHILDREN'S STRESSORS

With or without PTSD, childhood is full of normal stressors, including developmental stressors, such as toilet training, the first day of school, and puberty, and situational stressors, such as moving and going to a new school. The way your child copes with these stressors can affect her development and the way she handles subsequent life events. Coping mechanisms vary, depending on your child's developmental level, helpful resources, situation, lifestyle, and previous experience with stressful events.

Stress affects children as it does adults. Children have a variety of innate and acquired coping skills or strategies, including positive ones such as talking to a friend, crying, using humor, and playing, and not so positive ones such as yelling and tantruming. Children must learn to cope with fear, a normal emotional reaction to a specific real or perceived danger. Children perceive this hazard to be larger than themselves and thus a threat. Most childhood fears are limited and outgrown; some fears are realistic and persist into adulthood, such as fear of physical danger and bodily harm.

Some stressors are universal to all children; others are age specific. Illness and hospitalization are stressful to all children, regardless of age. Exposure to violence—in the family, in the community, or in the media—places significant stress on children of all ages. Discover the stressors that can affect your child so that you can minimize their effect.

Toddlers

It's hard to believe that young children experience stress. But the normal demands of growing up together with the pressures most families experience disallow a stress-free existence for most young children. Little stressors are beneficial because they teach toddlers to cope, but excessive stress is harmful, and your toddler is especially vulnerable because of his limited coping abilities.

Sources of stress for your toddler:

- Fear of losing his newly developed skills
- Having his rituals taken away; change in daily structure or disruption of family routines
- Separation from parents or parental loss (divorce, death, jail)
- New sibling
- Strangers
- Bedtime (can be viewed as separation from parents)
- Loss of security object (favorite blanket, doll)
- Overstimulation (too much commotion at once, such as a family reunion)

Your toddler may cope with stress by using infantile motor activities (rocking, restlessness, changing positions to move away from stressor) until he begins to use other strategies, such as play. Play serves as a stress relief method for toddlers. He can get out his frustrations and anxieties by banging on drums, working with a play hammer and nails, or molding clay. Your toddler will also hug his favorite toy, throw tantrums, suck his thumb, and even withdraw and become quiet.

Preschoolers

Due to the magical thinking during this stage, your preschooler faces many unique stressors. Some are due to his own distinctive understanding of the world, such as his fears; others are imposed, including those at preschool. Preschool stressors include:

- Separation from parents creates less stress than it did when he was a toddler, but it still persists, and seems to increase for a while around age 6.
- Being mocked or insulted by others. Despite the fact that he may like to insult others to boost his own self-image, your preschooler doesn't like to be on the receiving end of such comments.
- Having his questions go unanswered. Your enterprising preschooler asks constant questions, especially "Why," and he easily becomes upset if you do not respond or know the answer.
- Decreased attention. Your preschooler likes to talk, and he can become frustrated if ignored or put off.

Your preschooler may attempt to handle stress in a variety of ways, including occasionally lapsing into babyish behaviors such as thumb sucking or bed wetting. He may also develop unsightly nervous habits such as nail biting, hair pulling, nose picking, or masturbation.

School-Age Children

Today's school-age child has more stressors than ever, and your child is no exception. He is pressured by friends to be like them and do what they do and by you to excel in school and do extra-curricular activities. Extracurricular activities (sports, clubs, scouts, dance classes, karate) themselves can be stressful, espe-cially if they take up much of his free time. Being out in the world more than when he was younger exposes him to more violence. The school environment creates stress to his self-image as he competes for grades and teacher recognition, and he is probably worried about being asked to smoke cigarettes, drink alcohol, take drugs, or steal.

Your child may be pressured to think, feel, and behave at a level of maturity far beyond what should be expected of him. He may have adult responsibilities, like watching young siblings or cooking meals, or he may be making decisions that he's not really capable of making. Your child may even have little time for being a child and enjoying the spontaneous activities of childhood. General sources of stress for school-age children are:

- Starting school may be his first experience with being away from home all day. He may be fearful of getting lost or making an embarrassing social mistake. Help him cope by being there that first day, and showing him the ropes.
- Long vacations mean extended time away from peers. Friends are important at this age, and your child may fear losing them by his absence. Minimize this by allowing him to keep in touch with postcards or e-mail.
- Moving signifies changes in both school and peer group, both very stressful. He'll need to adjust to both losing old friends and making new ones.
- Change in family structure (divorce, remarriage) is an all-too-common stressor. Your child's ability to cope depends on a number of factors.
- Believe it or not, Christmas is just as much a stressor for children as it is for you.
- During puberty, preteens, especially girls, may become self-conscious regarding obvious signs of sexual development.

Your school-aged child uses a number of coping mechanisms to deal with stress. Some of these are unconscious, such as denial and reaction formation. Denial temporarily allows your child to deny that the stressor occurred in the first place. Reaction formation allows him to act or say the opposite of how he actually feels. For example, if your child is afraid, he may say something like, "I'm not afraid of anything. I'm the bravest one in this whole room." These mechanisms are healthy and normal, but help your child learn more age-appropriate coping mechanisms, such as communication and problem solving when he is ready.

Adolescents

Adolescence itself is stressful because of all its physical and psychological changes. Add the stresses of relationships, school, competition, and the uncertainty of what lies ahead, and it can easily be a time of stress overload. Your teen also needs to become less dependent on you and learn to make her own decisions. Sources of adolescent stress are:

- Pregnancy
- Peer loss
- Breakup with boy-/girlfriend
- Parental loss (divorce, death, jail), or death of other loved one
- School demands or frustrations
- Changes in his or her body and/or negative thoughts or feelings about him-/herself
- Having too many activities or having too high expectations

Adolescents have a variety of coping mechanisms. One is mastery whereby the teenager attempts to learn as much as possible about the situation. They can then use their problem-solving skills to work through the situation. By using conformity, your teen attempts to mirror the actions and appearance of his friends. Controlling behavior allows him to be in charge of some aspects of his life, and he will not accept parental or school rules without questioning them. Young teens use fantasy and rely on motor activities, such as sports, dancing, or other high-energy activities, as very effective tension-relieving strategies.

Adolescents may react negatively to stress by acting out, blaming others for their mistakes or problems, or by using drugs and alcohol. Therefore, it's helpful to teach your teen healthy stress management techniques before they feel overwhelmed by stress.

SIGNS OF STRESS IN CHILDREN

All Ages:
- *Sleep problems*
- *Changes in eating habits*
- *Frequent colds*

Ages 1 to 5:
- *Excessive clinging or crying*
- *Regressed behavior (goes back to wanting a bottle)*
- *Severe sensitivity to loud noises*
- *Irritability*
- *Trembling*

Ages 5 to 12:
- *Vague physical complaints*
- *Refusal to go to school*
- *Easily distractible*
- *Poor school performance*

Ages 12 to 14:
- *Isolates from family and friends*
- *Feels sad or depressed*
- *Aggression*

Ages 14 to 18:
- *Same as ages 12 to 14*
- *Antisocial behavior (fights, stealing)*
- *Night fears*

STRESS MANAGEMENT FOR CHILDREN

Stress management is important for all children, but especially important for those with PTSD. But do realize that your child can't manage his stress unless you manage yours, so make sure to keep your own stressors under control.

Healthy Lifestyle

Your child can deal better with stress when she has proper nutrition, plenty of exercise, and adequate sleep and rest. A healthy diet gives your child the energy she needs to draw on when she's stressed. It also enhances feelings of self-control and self-esteem. Make sure she stays away from caffeine, which can make her jittery, irritable, and unable to sleep. You say your 10-year-old doesn't drink coffee or tea? Great, but caffeine is also found in chocolate, cola, and other soft drinks, and many over-the-counter medications including cough syrups.

Exercise eases anxiety and leaves your child feeling more relaxed and energetic. Active children react less to stress and have a greater sense of wellness. So if your child is a couch potato, get him up and moving. Let him walk or bike safe distances; don't drive him. Encourage outdoor activities instead of TV watching or Internet surfing. Plan family bike outings or hikes.

The lack of sleep can be both the cause and the effect of stress. If your child does not get adequate sleep, his mental and physical processes deteriorate, leaving him with headaches,

What Nurses Know . . .

Suggestions for healthy eating for your child:
- *Substitute water and milk instead of sugary fruit drinks and sodas.*
- *Provide five servings of fruits and vegetables a day.*
- *Choose healthy sources of protein, such as lean meat, nuts, and eggs.*
- *Serve whole-grain breads and cereals.*
- *Broil, grill, or steam foods.*
- *Limit fast food and junk food.*

forgetfulness, the inability to concentrate, and irritability. Ample sleep improves his mood, fosters his feeling of competence, and provides him with optimal mental and physical functioning. To prevent or stop sleep problems, set regular bedtimes and provide a consistent, soothing bedtime routine such as reading. If he's still sleepy, make his bedtime earlier.

Teens need more sleep than school-age children. During this period, rapid growth, overexertion in activities, and a tendency to stay up late commonly interfere with sleep and rest requirements. In an attempt to "catch up" on missed sleep, your teenager may sleep late at every opportunity. Help your teen develop a steady sleep schedule that includes brief afternoon naps if necessary. Discourage sleeping more than two extra hours over the weekend. Staying in bed until the afternoon is equivalent to jet lag, leaving him even more sluggish and likely unable to fall asleep the next night.

Support

Your child needs to share her joys, fears, and frustrations. It's crucial for her to experience a secure parent–child relationship. This, along with a sense of worth and lovableness, serves as a foundation for effective coping. Talk with her and provide the support she needs. Despite all her protests, she still needs and wants your love, attention, and support.

Encourage your child to develop a strong friendship network, especially in his teens. A teenager needs friends he can count on for emotional support, feedback, and caring. Doing something with people he enjoys is a great way to help him refocus, and he'll realize that his friends have many of the same stressors that he has. Together they can come up with a variety of ways to beat stress.

Time Management

Time crunches create stress for almost everyone, including children whose lives are busier than ever. Your child may feel that she never has enough time to do all the things she has to do, causing her to feel overwhelmed. Learning time management is critical to managing day-to-day stress:

- Set priorities. If your child is overbooked with school work, clubs, sports, family responsibilities, and other time consumers, help him prioritize his activities and focus only on those that are important.
- Break up long-term goals into short ones, and write them down. Have your child break up large homework assignments, such as papers, reports, and projects, into small, manageable chunks, then write down what she has to do.
- Keep a calendar. Using a pocket or wall calendar, have your child keep track of all his assignments, extracurricular activities, family responsibilities, and social activities. Use different color inks for each category of activity for easier tracking. Once you create the calendar, study it to see if it is realistic. Can all these activities be done in their allotted timeframes, and still allow for personal time, relaxation, and "the-unexpected-and-time-consuming-stuff-that-just-happens"? If not, you both may need to rethink the schedule or discontinue some activities.
- Allow time each day for all that "unexpected-and-time-consuming-stuff-that-just-happens." Mistakes, interruptions, and unanticipated events always happen at the worst possible moment. Plan extra time so that your child will have time to deal with the unexpected.
- Encourage your child to visualize her goals. Have her "see" the finished paper or project in her mind. Mental rehearsals enable children to reach their goals more smoothly.
- Discourage procrastination. Have him do unpleasant tasks first and get them out of the way. Then let him work on the project he enjoys. It also helps to analyze why your child procrastinates. If he hates tidying up his room, help him find ways to make it more pleasant. Perhaps he and his friends can

join together to have cleaning parties at each other's homes to help clean each other's rooms.

- Tell her it's okay to say "no." Some children find it difficult to turn down opportunities or friends. Let her know that she doesn't have to please everybody or do everything. And be a good role model by learning to say "no" yourself.
- Encourage him to take breaks. Let him have a breather in between tasks and every 20 minutes when doing homework.

Humor

Laughter is the best medicine, even for children. Laughter defuses anger, increases alertness, decreases depression, improves mental health, and may even prevent disease. A hearty chuckle elevates the heart rate, aids digestion, eases pain, and releases endorphins, the pain-inhibiting brain hormones. Once a good laugh is over, your muscles relax and your pulse and blood pressure dip below normal. You're relaxed.

Humor is a great way to cope with stress—it's hard to hurt when you smile. But today's children are so busy growing up that they have little time for laughter. Foster play for the sake of playing and having fun, not competition. Play with them, and be silly. Wear clown noses or crazy hats; watch a funny movie together. Cartoons can be therapeutic. Have a funny-face making contest so he can win a tempting treat. Share jokes. Blow magic bubbles and let the aches sail away. Smile when you feel tense or down, and encourage your children to do the same.

Hobbies and Extracurricular Activities

Hobbies, clubs, sports, scouts, and other activities are great stress busters. When your child is busy and feeling a sense of accomplishment, he's on his way to dealing with stress. Activities can be done solo, with friends, or with a large group of people, just as long as the goal is to be involved in something he likes that will relieve tension. Remember, the activity should relieve stress, not cause it. Avoid overscheduling, and allow plenty of time for unstructured play.

Need ideas? How about: after-school clubs, Girl or Boy Scouts, 4H Clubs, and school or local sports clubs. Older children and teens enjoy hobbies and collections, traditional ones such as stamp, doll, card, and coin collecting, or more unique ones such as Pez dispenser, bottle cap, or rock collecting. Check to see if your church or synagogue has youth activities. Encourage volunteering to both relieve stress and help others. Last but not least, foster old-fashioned activities such as knitting, needlework, woodwork, and pet care.

Exercise

Regular exercise not only prevents stress, it also helps manage it. Exercise helps your body to release endorphins, giving you a feeling of calmness and well-being. The body releases endorphins both during and after exercise, which helps to relieve stress for a while. Vigorous activity helps release muscle tension, making it a natural outlet when your child's body is in a "fight-or-flight" state of response.

Encourage moderate, low-intensity, and aerobic exercises. Aerobic exercise involves sustained, large muscle group activity and requires deep breathing, which in itself can reduce stress. Examples include running, swimming, bicycling, brisk walking, and cross-country skiing. Moderate, low activity exercises are less vigorous than aerobic ones, but they still relieve stress while adding to strength and flexibility. Low-intensity exercises may be best as starters if your child has been a couch potato.

Relaxation Techniques

Useful in reducing the endocrine effects of chronic stress, relaxation techniques can decrease the stress response and elicit the relaxation response. The relaxation response is a state characterized by a feeling of warmth and quiet mental alertness. Relaxation techniques slow the heart rate and blood pressure, slow metabolism, and increase the blood flow to the brain and skin. They need to be practiced regularly, until your child feels comfortable with them. He should feel relaxed and refreshed after each session. If one technique doesn't work after he's used it for a reasonable period, try another.

Relaxation requires cooperation so set the mood with easy listening music. Small children can cuddle a favorite soft toy while being rocked gently. Older children can use deep breathing and muscle relaxation techniques.

For deep breathing, have your child close her eyes or look at an appealing item such as a toy or poster. Then have her take slow deep breaths in and out in a rhythmic manner. You may want to count out loud to keep her focused on the breaths instead of the stress.

Your child can learn progressive muscle relaxation if you treat it as a game. He could become the Amazing Shrinking Hero who shrinks his body bit by bit to squeeze into tiny places to save the world. Your hero gets to rest after his hard work by letting him muscles relax back to normal size. Any game will do as long as it uses the techniques that result in relaxation:

- Start with a comforting environment—a quiet room or soft music.
- Have your child lie on his back. Tell him to feel relaxed.
- Ask him to tighten one specific group of muscles (a hand, his face, a foot, etc.) for about five seconds.
- Now tell him to relax that muscle group and think about how it feels.
- Continue this process until all muscle groups have been relaxed.
- Make sure that he is in a well-supported, comfortable position. He may prefer to keep his eyes open through the whole process. He probably doesn't want to miss anything.

Guided imagery uses your child's natural imagination and experiences to allow him to concentrate on one or more mental images. It works best when incorporating as many of the five senses as possible and can even be used with imaginative tots.

Imagery should be fun. Allow your child to dream up his own images, real or imagined. He can be the center of attention as everyone stops to admire his sand castle on the beach. Or he could be the brave scientist who destroys the bad germs that make people sick. If your child can't come up with any images, help him by talking about his favorite things—a super hero, TV show, story, sport, vacation, pet, holiday, or season. You can also ask him to make three wishes and then guide him through one or all of them.

OTHER STRESS BUSTERS

- *Encourage your child to cuddle with a pet. Pets offer unconditional love and companionship. They can lift and soothe your child's spirits, and they can lower your child's stress response.*
- *Have your child listen to music.*
- *Let him draw.*
- *Inspire your child to write.*
- *Allow her to talk it out. Don't force her, but give her the opportunity.*
- *Discourage the use of tobacco, alcohol or drugs.*
- *Help him to replace negative thoughts with positive ones.*

Glossary

Abstinence: For the purpose of this book, this means not drinking any alcoholic beverage, including beer, wine, and hard liquor.

Acute: Sudden illness of short duration that is rapidly progressive and usually in need of urgent care.

Addiction: Habitual use of drugs, alcohol, or other substances, and characterized by uncontrolled cravings, tolerance, and symptoms of withdrawal when the substance is denied.

Adrenaline: Also called epinephrine; this is a hormone produced by the adrenal gland. It increases the heartbeat, strengthens the force of the heart's contraction, opens up the tiny tubes in the lungs plus numerous other effects. Adrenaline is part of the "fight-or-flight" reaction we have in response to being frightened.

Affect: How you display your emotional state; for example, looking sad and crying when depressed.

Alcoholism: A chronic, progressive, and potentially fatal disorder caused by both genetic and environmental factors that is characterized by tolerance and physical dependence, the inability to control drinking behavior, and personality changes and social consequences.

Anorexia nervosa: An eating disorder characterized by weight loss of usually greater than 15% of body weight, emaciation, thinking one is fat when actually very thin, and a fear of weight gain that results in self-imposed starvation.

Anxiety disorder: A group of disorders that includes PTSD, panic disorder, obsessive-compulsive disorder, phobia, or generalized anxiety disorder in which anxiety is a predominant feature.

Assessment: An evaluation that includes an interview, observation, and testing to develop a diagnosis and treatment plan.

Binge drinking: Generally refers to the consumption of four or more drinks in about 2 hours.

Bipolar disorder: Formerly known as manic-depressive illness, this is actually a group of mood disorders characterized usually by alternating episodes of depression.

Cognitive: The process of being aware, knowing, thinking, learning, and judging.

Cognitive behavioral therapy (CBT): A type of talk-therapy that focuses on beliefs and behaviors with the goal of replacing maladaptive behaviors, thoughts, and beliefs with more adaptive ones.

Comorbid: Simultaneous existence of a disorder (e.g., PTSD) interacting with one or more independent disorders (e.g., depression, substance abuse). Comorbidity worsens other conditions, complicates treatment, and interferes with functioning in age-appropriate social roles.

Conduct disorder: Repetitive and persistent pattern of behavior in which a minor violates the basic rights of others or age-appropriate norms or rules. Behaviors may involve aggression to other people or animals, the deliberate destruction of property, deceitfulness or theft, and serious violations of rules.

Cortisol: The main stress hormone in humans.

Depression: A mood disorder characterized by sadness, inactivity, difficulty with thinking and concentration, a significant increase or decrease in appetite and time spent sleeping, feelings of dejection and hopelessness, and sometimes suicidal thoughts.

Diagnosis: Process of identifying disease status by evaluating signs and symptoms.

Diagnostic and Statistical Manual of Mental Disorders, Fourth Edition, Text Revised (DSM-IV-TR): The official manual of mental health problems created by the American Psychiatric Association (APA) to understand and diagnose a mental health problem.

Domestic violence: Also called intimate partner violence (IPV), domestic violence includes actual or threatened physical, sexual, psychological, or emotional abuse between adults.

Flashback: A memory is suddenly and unexpectedly revisited.

Glucose: The simple sugar that serves as the chief source of energy in the body.

Grief: The normal process of reacting to a loss, which may be physical (such as a death), social (such as divorce), or occupational (such as a job). Emotional reactions of grief can include anger, guilt, anxiety, sadness, and despair. Physical reactions of grief can include sleeping problems, changes in appetite, physical problems, or illness.

Group therapy: Psychiatric care in which several patients meet with one or more therapists at the same time. The patients form a support group for each other as well as receiving expert care and advice. The group therapy model is particularly appropriate for psychiatric illnesses that are support intensive, such as anxiety disorders, but is not well suited for treatment of some other psychiatric disorders.

Heavy drinking: The National Institute on Alcohol Abuse and Alcoholism (NIAAA) defines heavy drinking as four or more drinks in a day (for women), consumed at least occasionally.

Hormone: A chemical substance produced in the body to control and regulate the activity of certain cells or organs.

Hyperarousal: A state of increased psychological and physiological tension characterized by such effects as exaggeration of startle responses, insomnia, fatigue, and accentuation of personality traits.

Hypervigilance: Abnormally increased arousal, responsiveness to stimuli, and screening of the environment for threats.

Impulsivity: Failure to resist an impulse, drive, or temptation to perform an act (e.g., an angry outburst, inappropriate touching) in a situation that may be damaging to the person or others.

Incidence: The rate at which new events occur in a population.

Learning disabilities: Identified difficulties with reading, writing, spelling, computing, or communication that affect people's ability to either interpret what they see and hear or to link information from different parts of the brain.

Major depressive disorder: A disorder is characterized by a depressed mood or a loss of interest or pleasure in daily activities consistently for at least 2 weeks.

Mental retardation: A disorder characterized by a significantly below-average score on a test of intellectual ability and limitations in such areas as self-direction, school, work, leisure activities, daily living, and social and communication skills..

Neglect: Failure to provide needed, appropriate care although financially able to do so, or when offered financial or other means to do so; this includes physical neglect (e.g., deprivation of food, clothing, shelter), medical neglect (e.g., failure to provide a child with access to needed medical or mental health treatments or to consistently administer prescribed medications), and educational neglect (e.g., withholding a child from school, failure to attend to special education needs).

Neurotransmitter: A chemical that is released from a nerve cell, which thereby transmits an impulse from a nerve cell to another nerve, muscle, organ, or other tissue.

Numb: Being emotionally unresponsive; indifferent.

Oppositional defiant disorder (ODD): A recurring pattern of negative, hostile, disobedient, and defiant behavior in a child or adolescent, but there is no serious violation of the basic rights of others.

Phobia: An unreasonable fear of an object or event that can cause avoidance and panic.

Physical abuse: Actual or attempted infliction of bodily pain and/or injury, including the use of severe corporal punishment. Physical abuse is characterized by physical injury (for example, bruises and fractures) resulting from punching, beating, kicking, burning, or otherwise harming a child.

Posttraumatic stress disorder (PTSD): A common anxiety disorder that develops after exposure to a terrifying event or ordeal in which grave physical harm occurred or was threatened.

Prevalence: The proportion of individuals in a population having a disease.

Protective factors: Factors that reduce risk of disease or disorder. Examples include a stable home and family support.

Psychiatry: Medical specialty concerned with the prevention, diagnosis, and treatment of mental illness. Psychiatrists are physicians.

Psychological maltreatment: Also called emotional abuse, psychological maltreatment includes acts or omissions by parents or caregivers that have caused, or could cause, serious behavioral, cognitive, emotional, or mental disorders.

Psychology: Study of the mind and mental processes, especially in relation to behavior.

Psychotherapy: Treatment of a behavior disorder, mental illness, or any other condition by psychological means; also called "talk therapy."

Random: The process by which an outcome is determined solely by chance, such as a coin flip.

Rape: Forced sexual intercourse; sexual assault. Legal definitions of rape may also include forced oral sex and other sexual acts.

Reflex: A physical reaction that is involuntary, such as sneezing.

Risk factors: Traits or habits that make a person more likely to develop disease or to engage in a potentially harmful behavior.

Schizophrenia: Brain disorder usually diagnosed during the teen or early adult years. The symptoms of schizophrenia are usually divided into two categories: positive and negative. "Positive" refers to overt symptoms that should not be there, such as delusions and hallucinations. "Negative" refers to a lack of characteristics that should be there. Negative symptoms include emotional flatness, inability to start and complete tasks, brief speech that lacks content, and lack of pleasure or interest in life.

Separation anxiety: Child experiences anxiety when separated from the primary caregiver (usually the mother). Separation anxiety is normal between 8 months of age and may last until 14 months old. This is different from Separation Anxiety Disorder.

Sexual abuse: Includes a wide range of sexual behaviors that take place between a child and an older person. Behaviors abusive often involve bodily contact, such as in the case of sexual kissing, touching, fondling of genitals, and intercourse. However, behaviors may be sexually abusive even if they do not involve contact, such as in the case of genital exposure ("flashing"), verbal pressure for sex, and sexual exploitation for purposes of prostitution or pornography.

Shell shock: The World War I name for what is known today as posttraumatic stress.

Social phobia: Excessive fear of embarrassment in social situations. This fear can have debilitating effects on personal and professional relationships.

Stress: A physical, chemical, or emotional factor that causes bodily or mental tension. Stress is a normal part of life that can help us learn and grow.

Syndrome: A set of signs and symptoms that tend to occur together and that reflect the presence of a particular disease or an increased chance of developing a particular disease.

Terrorism: The U.S. Department of Defense defines terrorism as "the calculated use of violence or the threat of violence to inculcate fear, intended to coerce or to intimidate governments or societies in the pursuit of goals that are generally political, religious, or ideological."

Torture: An act by which severe pain or suffering, whether physical or mental, is intentionally inflicted on a person.

Trauma: An injury, physical or emotional, that is emotionally painful, distressful, or shocking, which often results in lasting mental and physical effects.

Trauma reminders: People, places, activities, internal sensations, or other things that trigger memories of a trauma experience.

Withdrawal: Group of symptoms that may occur from suddenly stopping the use of an addictive substance such as alcohol after chronic or prolonged ingestion.

Developed from Emedicine Glossary of Terms for Posttraumatic Stress Disorder: www.emedicinehealth.com/post-traumatic_stress_disorder_ptsd/glossary_em.htm

Medline Plus/Merriam Webster: www.merriam-webster.com/medline plus

National Child Traumatic Stress Network (NCTSN): www.nctsn.org/about-us/who-we-are

Substance Abuse and Mental Health Services Administration: www.samhsa.gov

PTSD Resources

National Center for PTSD
www.ptsd.va.gov

Air Force Palace HART
Phone: 800-774-1361
Email: severelyinjured@militaryonesource.com

American Love and Appreciation Fund (for veterans)
Phone: 305-673-2856

Army Wounded Warrior Program
Phone: 800-237-1336 or 800-833-6622

DHSD Deployment Helpline
Phone: 800-497-6261

Marine for Life
Phone: 866-645-8762
Email: injuredsupport@M4L.usmc.mil

Military One Source
Phone: 800-342-9647
Website: http://www.militaryonesource.com/

Military Severely Injured Center
Phone: 800-774-1361
Email: severelyinjured@militaryonesource.com

National Coalition Against Sexual Assault
Phone: 717-728-9764

National Alliance for Mentally Ill
Phone: 800-950-6264

National Mental Health Association
Phone: 800-969-6642

Navy Safe Harbor
Phone: 800-774-1361
Email: severelyinjured@militaryonesource.com

Operation Comfort (for veterans and their families)
Phone: 866-632-7868 (1-866-NEAR TO U)

PTSD Information Hotline
Phone: 802-296-6300

PTSD Sanctuary
Phone: 800-THERAPIST

Rape, Abuse and Incest National Network
Phone: 800-656-HOPE Website: http://www.rainn.org

Crime Victim Compensation Programs

National Association of Crime Victim Compensation Boards
(NACVCB)
P.O. Box 16003
Alexandria, VA 22302
(703) 313-9500
www.nacvcb.org

STATE AND TERRITORY CRIME VICTIMS PROGRAMS

Alabama
(334) 242-4007
Alaska
(907) 465-3040

Arizona
(602) 364-1155

Arkansas
(501) 682-1020

California
(916) 323-3432

Colorado
(303) 239-4493

Connecticut
(860) 747-4501

Delaware
(302) 995-8383

D.C.
(202) 879-4216

Florida
(850) 414-3300

Georgia
(404) 559-4949

Guam
(671) 475-3324

Hawaii
(808) 587-1143
Idaho
(208) 334-6080

Illinois
(217) 782-7101/
(312) 814-2581

Indiana
(317) 232-1295

Iowa
(515) 281-5044

Kansas
(785) 296-2359

Kentucky
(502) 573-2290

Louisiana
(225) 925-4437

Maine
(207) 624-7882

Maryland
(410) 585-3010

Massachusetts
(617) 727-2200

Michigan
(517) 373-7373

Minnesota
(651) 282-6256

Mississippi
(601) 359-6766

Missouri
(573) 526-6006

Montana
(406) 444-3653

Nebraska
(402) 471-2828

Nevada
(702) 486-2740/
(775) 688-2900

New Hampshire
(603) 271-1284

New Jersey
(973) 648-2107

New Mexico
(505) 841-9432

New York
(518) 457-8727/
(718) 923-4325

North Carolina
(919) 733-7974

North Dakota
(701) 328-6195

Ohio
(614) 466-5610

Oklahoma
(405) 264-5006

Oregon
(503) 378-5348

Pennsylvania
(717) 783-5153

Puerto Rico
(787) 641-7480

Rhode Island
(401) 222-8590

South Carolina
(803) 734-1900

South Dakota
(605) 773-6317

Tennessee
(615) 741-2734

Texas
(512) 936-1200

Utah
(801) 238-2360
Vermont
(802) 241-1250

Virgin Islands
(340) 774-1166

Virginia
(804) 378-3434

Washington
(360) 902-5355

West Virginia
(304) 347-4850

Wisconsin
(608) 266-6470

Wyoming
(307) 777-7200

Bibliography

Advanced Abnormal Psychology Class at Appalachian State University in Boone, NC. (2005). *Posttraumatic stress disorder: A Web resource.* Retrieved from http://www1.appstate.edu/~hillrw/PTSD%20MM/PTSD_riskfactors.html

American Psychiatric Association. (2000). *Diagnostic and statistical manual of mental disorders* (Rev. 4th ed., text revision). Washington, DC: Author.

American Psychiatric Association. (2011). *Panic disorder. Healthy minds. Healthy lives.* Retrieved from http://www.healthyminds.org/Main-Topic/Panic-Disorder.aspx

Amstadter, A., Nugent, N., & Koenen, K. (2009). Genetics of PTSD: Fear conditioning as a model for future research. *Psychiatric Annals, 39*(6), 358-367.

Armour, M. (2003). Meaning making in the aftermath of homicide. *Death Studies, 27,* 519-540.

Beck, A., & Emery, G. (1991). *Anxiety disorders and phobias: A cognitive perspective. New York,* NY: Basic Books.

Brewerton, T. (2008). The links between PTSD and eating disorders. *Psychiatric Times, 25*(6), 1-7.

Brewin, C. R., Dalgleish, T., & Joseph, S. (1996). A dual representation theory of post-traumatic stress disorder. *Psychological Review, 103*, 670-686.

Brown, J. (2011). *Hormone linked to post-traumatic stress disorder, nature study shows.* University of Vermont. Retrieved from http://www.uvm.edu/research/?Page=news&storyID=116 31&category=uvmresearch

Butler, D., & Moffic, H. (1999). Post-traumatic stress reactions following motor vehicle accidents. *American Family Physician.* Retrieved from http://www.aafp.org/afp/990800ap/524.html

Campbell, J. (1972). *The hero with a thousand faces* (2nd ed.). Princeton, NJ: Princeton University Press.

Campbell, J. (2002). Health consequences of intimate partner violence. *The Lancet, 359*, 1331-1336.

Canadian Resource Centre for Victims of Crime. (2005). *The impact of victimization.* Retrieved from http://www.crcvc.ca/docs/victimization.pdf

Cohen, H. (2008). Psychotherapy treatment for PTSD. *Psych Central.* Retrieved from http://psychcentral.com/lib/2006/treatment-of-ptsd

Coleman, P. (2006). *Flashback.* Boston: Beacon Press.

Crenshaw, T. (2010). *Nightmares and PTSD: Research review. The National Center for PTSD. Retrieved from* http://www.ptsd.va.gov/professional/pages/nightmares_and_ptsd_research_review.asp

Defense Center for Excellence. (2009). *PTSD treatment options.* Retrieved from http://www.dcoe.health.mil/ForHealthPros/PTSDTreatmentOptions.aspx

Deykin, E. (2002). *Posttraumatic stress disorder in childhood and adolescence: A review.* Retrieved from www.medscape.com/viewarticle/430606

Downs, M. (2005). *Psychology vs. psychiatry: Which is better?* Retrieved from http://www.webmd.com/mental-health/features/psychology-vs-psychiatry-which-is-better

Ehlers, T., Halligan, S., & Clark, D. (2005). Unwanted memories of assault: What intrusion characteristics are associated with PTSD? *Behaviour Research and Therapy, 43,* 613-628.

EMDR Institute, Inc. (n.d.). *What is EMDR?* Retrieved from www.emdr.com/general-information/what-is-emdr/what-is-emdr.html

EMDR Network. (n.d.). *A brief description of EMDR.* Retrieved from www.emdrnetwork.org/description.html

Feeny, N., Zoellnre, L., Fitzgibbons, L., & Foa, E. (2000). Exploring the roles of emotional numbing, depression, and dissociation in PTSD. *Journal of Traumatic Stress, 13*(3), 489-498.

Finkelhor, D., Turner, H., Ormrod, R., Hamby, S., & Kracke, K. (2009). *Children's exposure to violence: A comprehensive national survey.* U.S. Department of Justice, Office of Justice Programs, Office of Juvenile Justice and Delinquency Prevention, NCJ 227744. Retrieved from www.ncjrs.gov/pdf-files1/ojjdp/227744.pdf

Fontaine, K. L. (2011). *Complementary and alternative therapies for nursing practice.* Upper Saddle River, NJ: Prentice-Hall.

Grinage, B. (2003). Diagnosis and management of post-traumatic stress disorder. *American Family Physician, 68*(12), 2401-2409.

Gore, A. (2011). Posttraumatic stress disorder. *Medscape.* Retrieved from http://emedicine.medscape.com/article/288154-overview

Grohol, J. (2009). *What is exposure therapy?* Retrieved from http://psychcentral.com/lib/2009/what-is-exposure-therapy

Gulliver, S., & Steffen, L. (2010). Towards integrated treatments for PTSD and substance use disorders. *PTSD Research Quarterly, 21*(2), 1-3.

Hackmann, A., Ehlers, A., Speckens, A., & Clark D. (2004). Characteristics and content of intrusive memories in PTSD and their changes with treatment. *Journal of Trauma Stress, 17*(3), 231-240.

Hamblen, J., & Stone, L. (2007). *What are the traumatic stress effects of terrorism?* National Center for PTSD. Retrieved from http://www.westga.edu/~vickir/PublicSafety/PS05%20 Training%20and%20Education/PS05situational_factors.pdf

Harman, R., & Lee, D. (2010). The role of shame and self-critical thinking in the development and maintenance of current threat in post-traumatic stress disorder. *Clinical Psychology and Psychotherapy, 17,* 13-24.

Harned, M., Rizvi, S., & Linehan, M. (2010). Impact of co-occurring posttraumatic stress disorder on suicidal women with borderline personality disorder. *The American Journal of Psychiatry, 167*(10), 1210-1217.

Harrer, M. E. (2009). Mindfulness and the mindful therapist: Possible contributions to hypnosis. *Contemporary Hypnosis, 26*(4), 234-244. doi:10.1002/ch.388

Herman, J. (1992). *Trauma and recovery.* New York, NY: Basic Books,

International Society of Traumatic Stress Studies. (2010). *Trauma and relationships.* Retrieved from http://www.istss. org/AM/Template.cfm?Section=PublicEducationPamphlets&T emplate=/CM/ContentDisplay.cfm&ContentID=1465

International Society of Traumatic Stress Studies. (2001). *Trauma and relationships. Mass disasters, trauma and loss.* Retrieved from http://www.istss.org/AM/Template.cfm?Section=Pu blicEducationPamphlets&Template=/CM/ContentDisplay. cfm&ContentID=1464

Iverson, K., Gradus, J., Resick, P., Suvak, M., Smith, K., & Monson, C. (2011). Cognitive-behavioral therapy for PTSD and depression symptoms reduces risk for future intimate partner violence among interpersonal trauma survivors. *Journal of Consulting and Clinical Psychology, 79*(2), 193-202.

Jeffreys, M. (2009). *Clinician's guide to medications for PTSD.* National Center for PTSD. Retrieved from http://www.ptsd. va.gov/professional/pages/clinicians-guide-to-medications- for-ptsd.asp

Ji, L., Xiaowei, Z., Chuanlin, W., & Wei, L. (2010). Investigation of posttraumatic stress disorder in children after animal- induced injury in China. *Pediatrics, 126*(2), 320-324.

Jülich, S. (2005). Stockholm syndrome and child sexual abuse. *Journal of Child Sexual Abuse, 14*(3), 107-129.

Karch, A. (2011). *2011 Lippincott's nursing drug guide.* Philadelphia: Wolters Kluwer/Lippincott, Williams & Wilkins.

Lanius, R., Williamson, P., Densmore, M., Boksman, K., Neufeld, R., Gati, J., & Menon, R. (2004). The nature of traumatic memories: A 4-T fMRI functional connectivity analysis. *American Journal of Psychiatry, 161*, 36-44.

Lasiuk, G., & Hegadoren, K. (2006). Posttraumatic stress disorder: Part I: Historical development of the concept. *Perspectives in Psychiatric Care, 42*(2), 13-19.

Lasiuk, G., & Hegadoren, K. (2006). Posttraumatic stress disorder: Part I: Development of the construct within the North American psychiatric taxonomy. *Perspectives in Psychiatric Care, 42* (2), 72-79.

Lubit, R. (2011). Posttraumatic stress disorder in children. *eMedicine.* Retrieved from http://emedicine.medscape.com/article/918844-overview

Mayo Clinic. (2009). *Drug addiction.* Retrieved from http://www.mayoclinic.com/health/drug-addiction/DS00183

Mayo Clinic. (2009). *Mental health: Overcoming the stigma of mental illness.* Retrieved from http://www.mayoclinic.com/health/mental-health/MH00076

Mayo Clinic. (2010) *Atypical antidepressants.* Retrieved from http://www.mayoclinic.com/health/Atypical-antidepressants/MY01561

Mayo Clinic. (2010). *Hypnosis.* Retrieved from www.mayoclinic.com/health/hypnosis/MY01020

Mayo Clinic. (2010). *Selective serotonin reuptake inhibitor (SSRI).* Retrieved from www.mayoclinic.com/health/ssris/MH00066

Memon, M. (2009). Brief psychotic disorder. *Medscape Emedicine.* Retrieved from http://emedicine.medscape.com/article/294416-overview

Miller, L. (2009) Family survivors of homicide. *American Journal of Family Therapy, 37*(1) 67-79.

Morland, L., Leskin, G., Block, C., Campbell, J., & Freidman, M. (2008). Intimate partner violence and miscarriage: Examination of the role of physical and psychological abuse and posttraumatic stress disorder. *Journal of Interpersonal Violence, 23*, 652–669.

Muscari, M. (2006). *Let kids be kids: Rescuing childhood.* Scranton, PA: University of Scranton Press.

National Cancer Institute. (2009). *Posttraumatic stress disorder.* Retrieved from http://www.cancer.gov/cancertopics/pdq/supportivecare/post-traumatic-stress/Patient/page2

National Center for Complementary and Alternative Medicine. (2011). http://nccam.nih.gov

National Center for PTSD. www.ptsd.va.gov

National Child Traumatic Stress Network. (2011). *Types of traumatic stress.* Retrieved from www.nctsn.org/trauma-types#q12

National Institute of Mental Health. (2010). *Post-traumatic stress disorder among adults.* Retrieved from http://www.nimh.nih.gov/statistics/1AD_PTSD_ADULT.shtml

National Institute of Occupational Safety and Health: Center for Disease Prevention and Control. (2008). *Workplace stress.* Retrieved from www.cdc.gov/niosh/blog/nsb120307_stress.html

National Institutes of Health. (2009). *Choosing a primary care provider.* Retrieved from http://www.nlm.nih.gov/medlineplus/ency/article/001939.htm

Nebraska Department of Veteran Affairs. (2007). *What is PTSD?* Retrieved from http://www.ptsd.ne.gov/what-is-ptsd.html#3

New York City Alliance on Sexual Assault. (2010). *Factsheets: PTSD and relationships.* Retrieved from http://www.svfreenyc.org/survivors_factsheet_107.html

Night Terrors Resource Center. www.nightterrors.org.

O'Connor, M. (2010). PTSD in older bereaved people. *Aging & Mental Health, 14*(6), 670–678.

Olatunji, B., Reese, H., Otto, M., & Wilhelm, S. (2008). Cognitive-behavioral therapy, behavioral therapy, and cognitive therapy.

In T. Stern, et al. (Eds.). *Massachusetts General Hospital comprehensive clinical psychiatry.* St. Louis, MO: Mosby Elsevier.

Pagel, J. (2000).Nightmares and disorders of dreaming. *American Family Physician.* Retrieved from http://www.aafp.org/afp/20000401/2037.html

Peterlin, B., Rosso, A., Sheftell, F., Libon, D., Mossey, J., & Merikangas, K. (2011). Post-traumatic stress disorder, drug abuse and migraine: New findings from the National Comorbidity Survey Replication (NCS-R*). Cephalalgia, 31*(2), 235-244.

Phillips, C., LeardMann, C., Gumbs, C., & Smith, B. (2010). Risk factors for posttraumatic stress disorder among deployed U.S. male Marines. *BMC Psychiatry, 10*(54). Retrieved from www.biomedcentral.com/content/pdf/1471-244X-10-52.pdf

Rauch, S. (n.d.). *Stress inoculation training (SIT) for post-traumatic stress disorder (PTSD).* Retrieved from www.therapyadvisor.com/LocalContent/adult/SITforPSTD.pdf

Rigoni, M. (2009). Grounding techniques explained. *Behavioral Health Resources.* Retrieved from http://www.bcbhr.org/Articles.aspx?7

Rizzolo, D., & Sedrak, M. (2010). Stress management: Helping patients to find effective coping strategies. *Journal of the American Academy of Physician Assistants, 23*(9), 20-24.

Rocha, L., Peterson, J., Meyers, B., Boutin-Foster, C., Charlson, M., Jayasinghe, N., & Bruce, M. (2008). Incidence of post-traumatic stress disorder (PTSD) after myocardial infarction (MI) and predictors of PTSD symptoms post-MI—A brief report. *International Journal of Psychiatry, 38*(3), 297-306.

Ruzek, J., Walser, R., Naugle, A., Litz, B., Mennin, D., Polusny, M.,...Scotti, J. (2008). Cognitive-behavioral psychology: Implications for disaster and terrorism response. *Prehospital Disaster Medicine, 23*(5), 397-410.

Sadock, B., & Sadock, V. (2007). *Kaplan and Sadock's synopsis of psychiatry: Behavioral sciences/clinical psychiatry* (10th ed.). Philadelphia: Lippincott Williams & Wilkins.

Seides, R. (2010). Should the current *DSM-IV-TR* definition for PTSD be expanded to include serial and multiple microtraumas as aetiologies? *Journal of Psychiatric & Mental Health Nursing, 17*(8), 725-731.

Sherman, M., Zanotti, D., & Jones, D. (2005). Key elements in couples therapy with veterans with combat-related posttraumatic stress disorder. *Professional Psychology: Research and Practice, 36,* 626-633.

Sheth, H., Zindadil, G., & Vankar, G. (2010). Anxiety disorders in ancient Indian literature. *Indian Journal of Psychiatry, 52*(3), 289-291.

Silva, R. (2004). *Posttraumatic stress disorder in children.* New York, NY: W.W. Norton.

Souza, T., & Spates, R. (2008). Treatment of PTSD and substance abuse comorbidity. *The Behavior Analyst Today, 9*(1), 11-26.

Stern, T., et al. (2008). *Massachusetts General Hospital comprehensive clinical psychiatry.* St. Louis, MO: Mosby Elsevier.

Tartakovsky, M. (2011). Tips for parenting with a mental illness. *Psych Central.* Retrieved from http://psychcentral.com/lib/2011/tips-for-parenting-with-a-mental-illness

Tobler, J. (n.d.). *Training teleconference: Mental health for military families: The path to resilience and recovery.* Resource Center to Promote Acceptance, Dignity, and Social Inclusion. Retrieved from www.stopstigma.samhsa.gov/teleconferences/archive/training/teleconference08032010.aspx

Trauma Center and Justice Center Resource. (n.d.). *First responders and traumatic events: Normal distress and stress disorders.* Retrieved from http://www.traumacenter.org/resources/pdf_files/First_Responders.pdf

Tufts University Family Medicine. (n.d.) *Sleep hygiene.* Retrieved from http://familymedicine.tufts.edu/pdf/Sleep-Hygiene.pdf

Tull, M. (2009). *Having emotional reactions to your emotions: Dealing with the experience of secondary emotions.* About.com. Retrieved from http://ptsd.about.com/od/selfhelp/a/secondary.htm

Tull, M. (2010). *Coping with your PTSD at work.* About. com. Retrieved from http://ptsd.about.com/od/selfhelp/a/ PTSDwork.htm

U.S. Department of Labor: Occupational Safety and Health Administration (OSHA). (n.d.). *Stress.* Retrieved from www. osha.gov/SLTC/etools/hospital/hazards/stress/stress.html

University of Maryland Medical Center. (n.d.). *Complementary medicine.* Retrieved from http://www.umm.edu/altmed

Vogler, C. (1998). *The Writer's journey: Mythic structure for storytellers and screenwriters.* Studio City, CA: Michael Wiese Productions.

WebMD. (2010). *Alcohol abuse and dependence symptoms.* Retrieved from http://www.webmd.com/mental-health/ alcohol-abuse/alcohol-abuse-and-dependence-symptoms

WebMD. (2011). *Prazolin for PTSD.* Retrieved from http://www. webmd.com/anxiety-panic/prazosin-for-ptsd

Whitlock, J. (2010). Self-injurious behavior in adolescents. *PLOS Medicine, 7*(5), 1-4.

Wohlfarth, T., Winkel, F.W., & van den Brink, W. (2002). Identifying crime victims who are at high risk for post traumatic stress disorder: Developing a practical referral instrument. *Acta Psychiatrica Scandinavica, 105,* 451-460.

Woord, S., Hall, R., Campbell, J., & Angott, D. (2008). Physical health and posttraumatic stress disorder symptoms in women experiencing intimate partner violence. *Journal of Midwifery Women's Health, 53*(6), 538-546.

Yellow Horse Brave Heart, M. (2005, May 23). From intergenerational trauma to intergenerational healing. *Wellbriety: White Bison's Online Magazine.* Retrieved from http://www. whitebison.org/magazine/2005/volume6/wellbriety!vol6no6. pdf

Index

American Psychological
    Association, 157
American Society of Internal
    Medicine, 152
Americans with Disabilities Act
    (ADA), 94
Amygdala, 27
Anger, 66
  components of, 184-185
  controlling, 186-189
  levels, variation in, 186
  PTSD partners with, 184-190
    conflict resolution, 189-190
  and victimization, 39
Anhedonia, 64
Anorexia nervosa, 87
Antianxiety medications, 126-127
  tips for taking, 127
Antidepressants, 120-122
Antipsychotics, 124-126
  for children, 210
  side effects of, 125
  tips for taking, 125-126
Anxiety, 13-16, 17
  level of, 14-15
Anxiety disorders, 16-17, 82-83
  in children, 205-207
Anxiety Disorders Association of
    America (ADAA), 16
Anxiolytics, 79
  signs of abuse and dependence, 80
Arnica, 137
Ativan (lorazepam), 126
Attention deficit hyperactivity
    disorder (ADHD), in
    children, 205
Atypical antidepressants, 122-124
Autonomic nervous system, 164
Avoidance, 61-63, 183
  dealing with, 63
  symptoms, 10-11
Awareness, balance, and connection
  in stress management, 171-172

Battle fatigue, 8, 36
Behavioral avoidance, 62

Beliefs, spiritual, 176
Bereavement, 44, 71, 197
Bipolar disorder, in children, 202
Board certification, 149
Body, response to stress, 25-28
Borderline personality disorder,
    73-77
  dealing with, 76-77
  symptoms of, 75
Boston Consortium Model:
    Trauma-Informed
    Substance Abuse Treatment
    for Women, 79, 81
Brain, response to stress, 25-28
Breathing
  deep, 223
  rapid, 84
  retraining, 111
Brief psychotic disorder, 19
Bulimia nervosa, 87

Cancer, and PTSD, 45
Cardiovascular effects of stress,
    167-168
Causes of PTSD, 24-34, 25
CDC Natural Disaster Resources, 102
Celexa (citalopram), 121
Chair massage, 134. *See also*
    Massage therapy
Chamomile, 140-141, 144
  cautions with, 141
CHAMPUS, 158
Chi, 138
Child neglect, 195
Children, 193-224
  expression of distress, 199-200
  possible associated problems,
    201-207
  relationship with, 91-93
    strengthening of, 92-93
  stress, 210-224
  treatment of, 207-210
  traumas, 194-197
Clinical social workers, 156
Cocaine, 80
  signs of abuse and dependence, 80